# A GLIMPSE THROUGH PURDAH

## Asian women – the myth and the reality

To Frank with love
~ kisses.

*[signature]*

# A GLIMPSE THROUGH PURDAH

## Asian women – the myth and the reality

*Sitara Khan*

**Trentham Books**

First published in 1999 by Trentham Books Limited

Trentham Books Limited
Westview House
734 London Road
Oakhill
Stoke on Trent
Staffordshire
England ST4 5NP

**British Cataloguing in Publication Data**
A catalogue record for this book is available from the British Library
ISBN 1 85856 054 3
(h/b ISBN 1 85856 117 5

Cover design by Aquarium Graphic Design

Designed and typeset by Trentham Print Design Ltd., Chester and printed in Great Britain by The Cromwell Press Ltd., Wiltshire

**Dedication to my parents:**
Mother: Her dainty fingers oiled
and tamed into plaits
that which the mother's milk'd nurtured.

Father; The man of vision searched
for English teachers for his daughter
even standing at bus stops.

## Acknowledgements

I am indebted to the people without whose help and unstinting support this book would not have been completed: Maura Chatterjee for typing the first draft of the book and invaluable discussions and Clive Brisco for his critical insights; Richard Hughes for his help in organising the material and acting as grammarian; my sister Shamshad Khan for her penetrating home truths and for letting me use two of her poems at the beginning and end of the book; the women I interviewed both in the Subcontinent and in Calderdale; my hosts in the Subcontinent, in particular my cousin Akhter and his wife Shanaz, and Freney Pochkanwalla as well as officials in LEAs for providing me with reports and other written and oral material; and Gillian Klein without whose encouragement and support writing for publication might not even have materialised.

# Contents

# Earthbound Traveller

From under a stone
from a bone (they say)
she rose.

Deep down
out of her black box
she's pink
unconfined flesh

drips
travels
spreads
released

earthbound traveller
wings strapped to my back
dreams
organza tied
with bootlaces.

Tell me who I'm not.
I'll tell you who I am
who I can
who I will be

how
by any other name
I struggle to be me.

From lands of many tongues
we're asked to speak only one.

They snaked their limits around us
bound us
tongues – tied – tightly

| | |
|---|---|
| Kyah? | (What?) |

tongues – tied – tightly

| | |
|---|---|
| Kyah? | (What?) |

Hush no
you don't say it like that.

You say it like this.

| | |
|---|---|
| Jerow(n) say ukhayr ker | (ripped from our roots) |
| mittee uddayr ker | (soil unravelled) |
| loat ayheh. | (we have returned) |
| Jerow(n) ko sambhaal ker | (Having settled our roots) |
| khwishay mittee main mila ker | (our hopes lost to the soil) |
| hum ugthay heh | (we grow) |

Jerow(n) say

| | |
|---|---|
| 'No say **roots**' | |
| Kyah? | (What?) |

'Roots'
**Roots** say ukayr ker
'No say **ripped from**'
Kyah?

'Ripped from'
**Ripped from our roots**
mittee uddayr ker

'No say soil torn'

What?
It doesn't mean that.

| | |
|---|---|
| Humaaray zabaano ko uddayr ker | (Having unravelled our tongues) |
| mittee may milah ker | (lost to the soil) |
| humaaray jerow(n) ko ukhayr ker | (having ripped out our roots) |
| humaaray zabaano ko kart ker | (cut our tongues) |
| zenjeeray say bandh ker | (tied us with chains) |
| Phir beh ham ugthay heh | (still we grow) |
| Phir beh ham urthay heh. | (still we fly). |

*Shamshad Kahn*

# Chapter 1
# Asian Women in the West

Threads: silver gold, cotton silk,
Weave me a veil.
Beauty masked, flesh protected,
Come with me and be in love.
Glimpses caught of shattered hopes,
Come! Fill my cup and be my love.

The person who passes for an Asian woman in the West somehow represents any or all of these populations and traditions; she could be a Portuguese-speaking Christian, French-speaking Hindu or Muslim from Mauritius, or an English-speaking Jain from the West Indies. Curiously enough, Chinese and Southeast Asian people are not included in this definition. The term 'Asian' arose during the early nineteen seventies in Britain when there was confusion about how to address people from India and Pakistan. This was further compounded by the break-up of Pakistan and the formation of Bangladesh as a separate state in 1971. At about the same time there was an increasing influx of people originally from the Subcontinent, who were being encouraged to leave Africa, culminating in the mass expulsions from Idi Amin's Uganda. Many found themselves in Britain, the US and Canada. Soon after their arrival, the all-encompassing term 'Asian' appears to have been coined to apply exclusively to people of the Indian Subcontinent and their descendents.

This book explores the lives of 'Asian' women on the Subcontinent and in the West. It shows how women's lives – like men's – are affected by history and politics, by class and economic position, by religious affiliation and family patterns. But unlike men, women are affected also by patriarchy and a traditional belief stretching back in time that it is appropriate for men – fathers, husbands, brothers – to control their lives. While many women internalise such oppression and are complicit in its perpetuation, others in both East and West struggle to control their own lives, with varying success.

This study of the educational and employment opportunities of samples of women in Karachi in Pakistan, Bombay in India, and Halifax in Britain draws out the similarities and differences in the experiences of Asian women who work for their living. The findings indicate that whereas women on the Subcontinent have to contend mainly with patriachy, in the West they have to face the additional obstacles to self-determination caused by racism.

One form of racism is the 'received wisdom' among Westerners by which they perceive Asian women according to a series of stereotypes. They are likely to see the role of Asian women as 'limited to the kitchen, the children and the religious rituals, and they are both emotionally and economically dependent on their husbands' (Carby, 1982). This book explores the myths and the realities on two · continents and discusses the customs that arouse greatest suspicion and alarm in the West: *purdah, sati* and *hareem.*

## Stereotypes of Asian women

The following stereotypes all have some currency in the West:

Asian women wear the veil and this is an integral part of their religion

They walk behind the men

Asian women come from a primitive backward culture

Asian languages lack the complexity of European languages, especially English, essential for rational thought

Their clothes are colourful and decorative, but not conducive to holding responsible professional positions

They find it difficult to adjust to living in Britain because they come from a hot country

They have greater health problems because they do not want to integrate

Asian women don't want to work

Asian women, especially Muslim women, are not allowed to work because of their religion

Asian women do not make any household decisions; all decision-making is left to the men

Asian women have no control of finances

Asian women accept their lot and do not struggle against the circumstances in which they find themselves

Asian women come from restrictive patriarchal families

Asian women have arranged (forced) marriages in which they are trapped

Asian women are passive victims of circumstance (Parmar, 1982)

Asian women are submissive (Lim, Tsutakawa and Donelly, 1989)

This feeling of helplessness is epitomised in the most barbaric of all cultural acts – that of *sati* (widow burning)

They are incapable of doing the things that white British women do

As their potential is severely limited there is no point in providing them with equal opportunities.

In fact, Asian women are not a monolithic group but come from diverse socio-political and cultural backgrounds with differing viewpoints and are far removed from the stereotype.

The position of Asian women in the West, specifically in one English town of high Asian settlement, is compared and contrasted with women in similar occupational areas in the Subcontinent. The bulk of the empirical research was carried out in Karachi in Pakistan and the rest in Bombay, Bangalore and Mysore in India, and in Halifax in England. The reason for dividing the work in this way was twofold: a) I was born in Karachi and spent my formative years there, so I had some background on which to draw; b) it provided an opportunity to see the extent to which Muslim women matched their Western stereotype of being hampered by purdah, veiling or female seclusion generally associated with them. The field work focused on women in teaching, retailing, finance and garment manufacturing.

I chose urban rather than rural settings because Asian women in the West are more likely to have roles similar to urban women in the Subcontinent (Allen and Wolkowitz, 1987, Commission for Racial Equality, 1988). Many of them had lived in British cities for at least two and in many cases for three or four generations. In Britain I chose Halifax, the administrative town of Calderdale where I had worked as an education officer for some nine years and came to know the community both professionally and socially. Women employees and service users of the voluntary and statutory sectors felt at ease about answering my questions candidly.

Whilst there is merit in studying the particular domestic or employment situation to confirm or refute the received wisdom in the West about Asian women in general and Muslim women in particular, concentrating on the woman hidden away in purdah or some innocent helpless victim dragged to her deceased husband's funeral pyre serves only to camouflage the underlying similarities in the position of women across socio-cultural and political boundaries. International comparisons show that women experience a host of common problems irrespective of the particular state ideology or economic system 'yet each country has distinctive social expectations and legal norms defining appropriate female activities and cultural values which affect women's aspirations for meaningful status inside and outside the home' (MacDonald, 1976). Women across the socio-economic and political divide are regarded as second-class citizens. Asian women in the West and in the Subcontinent share this status with their counterparts all over the world. As De Beauvoir observed, 'One is not born, but rather becomes a woman' as her realities are defined in terms of her relationship with male relatives: wife, sister, mother, daughter (quoted in Singh, 1993).

Assumptions about the status of women cannot be based merely on the level of industrialisation, nor can it be assumed that universal suffrage has allowed them to have greater participation in the public sphere, for example politics and the labour market. Capitalist, socialist and 'mixed' economies all reflect gender differentiation, beyond a few privileged women in prominent positions. On entry into Britain or other countries in the West, Asian women's experience is both the same as and different from that of women in the majority culture as they are cast in a set of racial stereotypes. The position of Asian women has been profoundly determined by European colonialism in the Subcontinent; the racist evolution of the colonial ideology continues to shape the policy and practice that affects their position in the West.

## British racism: a colonial legacy

The British colonisation of India which grew out of trade links with the Subcontinent from about the 1550s onwards evolved into a system of economic exploitation and political subjugation of a people. The economic undermining of the country's infrastructure, although varied, rested on two basic principles: the cheap supply of raw materials, especially produced for British industrial or domestic needs, and levying taxation on Indian products to reduce competition for British products sold in India. The political system was managed by introducing pro-Raj puppet *rajas* and *ranis* who acted as buffers between the British ruling elite and the mass of Indian people. Many of these *rajas* and *nawabs* were gradually introduced to and began to adopt a Western lifestyle. The English language, which finally replaced Urdu as the language of bureaucracy and government, coupled with the introduction of Western clothing for government departments such as the navy, army and civil service, became the emblems of the British presence in India. The English-speaking Indian bourgeoisie with Western education felt different from and superior to the indigenous population. No matter how hard its members tried to emulate the white *sahib*, however, they were confined to the clearly designated areas for the Indians. The racial apartheid was all-pervasive: it determined living accommodation and leisure as well as areas and levels of employment within any particular professional hierarchy. It became a matter of record that

4

women, many of whom had held prominent politico-economic positions before the colonial era, found themselves under increasing attack during the British Raj. Their right to govern was severely curtailed and their right to inherit property abolished, bringing it in line with the situation for women in Britain. Muslim women everywhere in the Subcontinent who had a right – at least in theory – to inherit property lost out more generally. Their Hindu counterparts who had similar rights in certain states like Malabar saw these eroded as the Raj sought the help and support of reactionary religious 'authorities' to sanction and maintain the most repressive elements of Islam and Hinduism. In consequence the incidence of purdah for Muslim women and sati for Hindu women increased, adding to the general undermining of the position of women and making it easy for the British to argue that the salvation of the nation in general and women in particular lay with their white rulers.

Women continued to lose out under the Raj as their rights to agricultural and other land were eroded. They were subjected to poor wages in factories and mines and bore the brunt of the policy of indentured labour which followed the abolition of slavery. Under this policy, Indian men were transported to Africa and other parts of the British empire to provide cheap labour or shortage skills, whilst the women were often left at home to support the family. Even when they did join their men they were at a disadvantage, for they were excluded from the job market and therefore took longer to familiarise with the customs of the countries in which they found themselves. This policy of transporting cheap labour to serve Britain's economic or political needs continued after the abolition of indentured labour in 1920 until well into the 1970s, culminating in the immigration to Britain of large numbers of people after the Second World War. But the story of Asian women's struggle throughout the colonial and neo-colonial period has largely remained untold. Their striving to support their families and challenge British colonialism in the Subcontinent and racist practices in Britain often goes unrecorded. It is important that these women should speak for themselves and that the history of their ongoing struggle should be documented.

British power in India, established by brute force and local acquiescence, lasted from the days of the East India Company in the seventeenth century until 1947, culminating in the partition of the Subcontinent into the political states of India and Pakistan, with the latter being further divided into East and West Pakistan, separated by some thousand miles. To control a land mass of 5,230,928 square kilometres, ranging from the highest mountains in the world to tropical desert conditions, with an equally diverse population, both racially and religio-culturally, was not an easy task. It was therefore simplified by a series of reductionist concepts. For example the subtle, complex political situation was simplistically portrayed as 'a country in disarray'; languages were treated as backward dialects; the religions and cultures were viewed as barbaric and oppressive, especially to women. From this point on, the white man's burden was clear: it was to bring a civilising influence to a backward culture in the form of teaching them the English language, style of dress and the only true religion – Christianity. It provided the intellectual and moral justification not only for colonialism, but also for the use of extreme force to maintain control. The white man, even if he was in fact darker than the white-skinned blue-eyed Kashmiris, was justified in feeling morally and racially superior. To teach the subjugated 'darker races' the civilised ways could be seen as desirable to all, including to potential critics of colonialism at home.

The colonisation of India, then, was originally justified to the British public on moral, rather than economic, grounds. It succeeded in creating an image of a culture in disarray, in particular the women who desperately needed rescuing by white lords and ladies. This image provided a smoke-screen, a camouflage, for the fact that the position of Asian women continued to decline during British colonialism in significant ways, such as loss of inheritance rights.

The old colonial way of thinking may have evolved but it remains essentially the same. The received attitude toward the Asian woman in the West including Britain in the 1990s is that she is the ignorant victim of a barbaric, oppressive, undemocratic culture. The burden for the modern white man is to educate and liberate her from the clutches of her culture. Another aspect of colonial thinking also prevails: the Asian woman is believed to have low educational and career aspirations, and to be incapable of achieving high status in the world of work. The research reported in the following pages presents quite another picture.

Chapter 2

# The history, geography and culture of the Indian Subcontinent

Snow-capped mountains, sun-scorched sands, gushing waters,
Echoing voices
domes and palaces treasures renew
Come with me and be in love.

The Koh-i-Noor diamond gleams in the royal crown, symbol of the prized jewel that the Indian Subcontinent was in the crown of the British Empire. Yet the prevailing view in the West in general and Britain in particular, is that it is a place of grinding poverty which lacks order and is always unbearably hot. Above all it treats women as second-class, as victims of an oppressive, uncivilised culture.

It is in order to demystify some of the received wisdom surrounding the Subcontinent and the role of women in particular that I begin with history. This chapter sets the context in which Asian women's lives are played out and how the past – the British colonial legacy – continues to affect the position of Asian women both in the Subcontinent and in the diaspora.

The Indian Subcontinent is a large peninsula covering some 5,230,928 square kilometers, including the small island of Sri Lanka. It has some of the coldest and the hottest temperatures in the world: in the Himalayan mountains in the north and to the south at the Equator, with desert areas in the west and low land to the east. In 1947, following independence from British colonial rule, the mainland was divided into two states, India and Pakistan, along religious lines, Hindu and Muslim respectively. East Bengal was a part of Pakistan which broke away in 1972 to form a separate nation, Bangladesh. The apparently clear-cut religious divide, however, conceals enormous religious and ethnic diversity in all three countries.

Christianity was introduced into the Subcontinent in about the fourth century AD; the influence of Europeans encouraged converts. Islam was brought to India with the invaders from Turkey and Afghanistan at the beginning of the eleventh century, making many converts from other religions. Jews came from about the second century AD; the oldest synagogue in the world still remains in south India, although the Jewish population has declined in recent years through emigration, mainly to Israel.

Buddhism originated in what is now Nepal, in the north-east of the Subcontinent, in the fifth century BC; and although now very much a minority religion, still has adherents. Zoroastrianism, still practised by the small community of Parsis based mostly around Bombay and Karachi, sprang up largely because of religious refugees from Persia who fled after the Arab conquest in the eighth century AD. Some ten million Indians, mostly originating from the Punjab, follow the Sikh religion, founded in the sixteenth century by Guru Nanak.

There are still several distinct racial groupings: pygmies in the Andaman and Nicobar Islands in the Bay of Bengal, Australoids and Mongoloids in the North-east who arrived millennia ago. There is also evidence of eastern Mediterranean people, especially in Gujerat and Maharashtra.

## Prehistory: 3000BC to 1st century BC

The Subcontinent has been the subject of political invasions, trade links and immigration for four and a half thousand years. All have left their mark on its languages, cultures, religions and racial composition, and indeed on the position of women, as this book reveals.

The earliest civilisations known to have existed on the Subcontinent, dating back to 3000 to 1700 BC, were those of Mohenjodaro in Sindh and Harappa in the Punjab (Tharu and Lalita, 1991). These resembled the civilisations of Mesopotamia and Egypt: there was evidence of brick buildings, statuettes in stone and metal, jewels, and knives and seals covered in as yet undeciphered pictorial motifs. The metals used were gold, silver, copper, tin and lead. There was spinning of wool and cotton, and growing of wheat and barley. These were fairly advanced urban civilisations, with underground drainage systems. What is unclear, because of the lack of sufficient written material, is the role women played. How the struggle for power resolved itself into gender relations and how they are enacted in the everyday lives of Asian women is the subject of scrutiny here. What the archaeological findings show is the presence of both male and female godheads.

Feminist historians have argued that in the Subcontinent as elsewhere in the ancient world, women shared political and economic power with men, and the godhead figurines were a symbolic representation of the gender relations of the time. Rosalind Miles (1989) argues that mother goddess ruled supreme but allowed the male gods to coexist without feeling a threat from their presence. There was a struggle for power and in the conflict women lost out, in the Subcontinent as elsewhere in the world. Whilst in some communities matrilineage is still occasionally found, this does not constitute matriarchy. This is clear from examples of other cultures such as the Jewish community, where religious affiliation is passed through the female but the power resides with the male. There seems to be consensus amongst historians that the Dravidian (indigenous Indian) women performed religious rites. These may have been shared with their male counterparts. The principle of female *shakti* or power has been recognised in the Subcontinent for millennia, argue Joanna Liddle and Rama Joshi (1986). Remnants of these concepts are evident in such deities as Kali. Kali, a metaphor for women, has the power both to give and take life. Women's involvement in the temple rituals is reflected in the present day idea of *sava dasi* or servant woman. She served the gods in a variety of ways which may have included singing and dancing; temple carvings point to this long tradition which is passed down to modern day India.

## Vedic period to Aryan invasion and rise of Hinduism

From the second millennium BC, the Harappan civilisation was overwhelmed by Indo-Aryan immigrants from central Asia. The Aryans, who were paler skinned than the indigenous Dravidians, introduced the caste system along racial and occupational lines. In this system race and occupation became inextricably linked, with the Aryans enjoying the upper echelons of society and the Dravidians relegated to less favourable positions. This was compounded by the introduction of an Aryan language which, over time, mingled with the indigenous languages to form Sanskrit. These processes affected women in at least two ways. As the religion and language of rituals were alien to the existing population, men of the invading group took over the religious duties, thus dislodging women from this esteemed role. Seclusion or *purdah* of upper-class women may also have been brought in by the Aryans, to ensure that only men of the designated priestly class could be charged with religious duties. Even though indigenous women of the lower-classes continued to offer their services to the deities in the form of dancing, both the act and the performer would have become devalued and in time disreputable. Once the superiority of the male was established, it was a logical progression to assume that a woman's life without her husband was meaningless. The burying of a chieftain's belongings and wives – an Indo-Aryan custom – was brought in to the Subcontinent, as was the seclusion of upper-class women which already operated in the Eastern Mediterranean. These practices ultimately evolved into *sati* and *purdah*, which are discussed in the next chapter.

## Mauyrua and Gupta period and the invasion of Alexander the Great

The Mauyrua and Gupta period is considered by many as a golden age in the history of the Subcontinent prior to the Moghul era. Broadly, it was characterised by religious and social tolerance. Women, along with men, challenged the religious orthodoxy of Hinduism, in which priestly and warrior classes held the power. 'Both the Buddhist and *bakhti* poetry came from a movement that opposed caste discrimination and the ritualised Hinduism of Brahmin priests' (Tharu and Lalita, 1991). This suggests that women had been accustomed to a greater degree of freedom before the Aryan invasion.

For several millennia, India has been a melting pot: people immigrated and invaded through the Himalayas and came to the western regions from the sea. One such was Alexander the Great, known in the Subcontinent as Sikander-e-Azam. All brought their own customs and traditions. Some may have reinforced existing ones; in other cases new customs would have been introduced. Veiling of women of noble birth was a Greek custom at the time, as it was in imperial Iran, a country Alexander the Great conquered in fourth century BC (L. Ahmed, 1992). It may equally well have reinforced an existing tradition in the Subcontinent or been introduced with other new customs.

## The Moghuls

The Moghul empire, founded by Genghis Khan's descendants in the thirteenth century AD, lasted eight hundred years, until defeated by invading Europeans. By the time they reached India, the Moghuls had adopted Islam. Notable Moghul emperors included Akbar the Great, who reigned from 1556-1605. Akbar united the country and created a climate of peaceful co-existence among the religious communities, in which arts and literature flourished. He sought to reconcile religious differences and even introduced a new religion, called Dein-I-Allahi. He married a Hindu and a Muslim wife to demonstrate his commitment to the principle of universality of the religious message.

From the time of the Mogul Emperor Baber (1483-1530), attempts were made to foster religious tolerance: one example was prohibiting the slaughtering of cows in India. The name of the Moghul Emperor Shah Jahan (1592-1666) is etched into the pages of world history, for building the Taj Mahal for his deceased wife Arjumand Bano, known as Mumtaz Mahel. This temple of love represents a typically Moghul synthesis of ideas, art and design drawn from both Hindu and Muslim cultural traditions. When the Taj Mahal was being built between 1632 and 1648 in India, England was a minor power, described by a Venetian ambassador as: 'useless to all the rest of the world, of no consideration' (Hill, 1991, quoted in A.S. Ahmed, 1993).

Referring to Murshadabad in 1757, Lord Clive, so-called Clive of India, said: 'This city is as populous and extensive as London. It contains beautiful buildings which rival the best in Europe and has more ambassadors in residence than London.' The Moghul empire survived in slow decline until 1857, when the British finally took the crown from the largely powerless Bahadur Shawzaffair. He was placed in solitary confinement and all his male descendants were beheaded.

The Muslims of the Moghul empire did not dismantle the already well-established caste system. Instead they introduced another layer of socio-political structure, beneath which existed the two Hindu and Muslim hierarchies. There were some attempts to outlaw, or at least keep in check, the practice of *sati*. The Muslims adopted the Subcontinent as their home; they were influenced by, and in turn influenced, the local customs. Purdah amongst upper- and middle-class Hindu women, for example, became more widespread as did the stricter Hindu attitude to divorce amongst Muslims. Both communities continued to have female queens, even if the overall empire was in the hands of male emperors. In addition, women were attached to Moghul courts as artists, including dancers.

Much of the secular literature of the later period can be traced to the patronage of the courts, especially the Moghul courts, which by all accounts had space for artists of various kinds in their entourages. The women's folk songs 'in nearly every region are sung mainly to celebrate the cycle of agricultural year, and have their sources in the local non-Aryan cultures' (Tharu and Lalita, 1991). During the British Raj, when the Moghuls lost power, many of the women artists who had been supported by the court became dispossessed.

Clearly India, the country the Europeans eventually colonised, was the opposite of a cultural desert. It was bustling with economic and cultural activity, a magnet for the trade the Europeans were so eager for. Indeed the earliest European traders were both awed and impressed by the culture they found; its subsequent impoverishment was due largely to the pillaging of their successors. Although 95 per cent of the Indian collection held by the Victoria and Albert Museum remains in store, enough is on display to indicate the fabulous wealth that India once enjoyed. Cultural centres like Lahore and Lucknow, with their legendary elegance and charm, like the other highly developed Indian cities of the Moghul and earlier eras, needed planners, architects, mathematicians, artisans and artists. Cross-fertilisation across the arts and sciences was regarded as natural, and everywhere there was a respect for learning which still persists in the Subcontinent today. One of the reasons for this respect both for knowledge and for the teacher was the method of transmitting knowledge orally. This meant that a close relationship was forged between teacher and pupil. The trust placed in the teacher was such that even in instances where strict purdah was observed, the rule was relaxed to accommodate a male teacher for female students. Indeed this still persists.

Women made their own contribution. For example, Noor Jehan, wife of the seventeenth century emperor Jahangir, was a cultured and powerful Persian woman who compensated for the erratic behaviour of her opium-addicted husband. She came to be known as the power behind the crown, who loved the arts and did much to develop Persian styles of the arts in the Moghul Empire. Her particular contributions, besides that of running the country, were to foster the delicate Persian style of jewellery which largely superseded earlier heavy styles, and to introduce rose perfume.

An arranged marriage system co-existed with love matches. The latter is nowhere more true than in the marriage of Shah Jahan and Mumtaz Mahel, immortalised in the Taj Mahal.

## European invasions and British colonisation

From the sixteenth century onward Europeans began to arrive in the Subcontinent, including the Portuguese, British, Dutch and French, all initially as traders, then as conquerors of territory. The British were the most successful.

Trade, which began in Bengal, was finally replaced by political control. Nawab Siraj Ud-daullah, the governor of Bengal and Orissa, was defeated by the British, who by 1790 effectively controlled the Subcontinent. Throughout the nineteenth century there were uprisings against the British Raj, the most well-known in 1857, which culminated in Independence in 1947. The history of women under the British is complex. The British establishment, aided by the Christian missionaries, saw itself as the liberator of Indian women. Their perception did not match reality as women's position continued to decline. Throughout the nineteenth century the national liberation movement became inextricably intertwined with the question of women's position.

## Intellectual justification for colonialism

Throughout the colonial period, from the eighteenth century onward, the Western powers needed intellectual as well as economic and political justification for their policies towards the countries they had occupied or wished to occupy. The process of colonisation required the agreement of the populations at home. If they could be convinced, as many still are, that these immensely profitable colonial adventures were also morally justified because of the inherently inferior morality of the 'natives', agreement was assured. The ideological benefit derived by the colonising nations was significant. People in Britain were socialised into accepting a world view in which '*Great* Britain was a dominant, unassailable power engaged in the glorious task of bringing civilisation to the 'natives' of the Empire; a task that was nothing less than her destiny.' (Wolpert, 1989). Nineteenth century European Intellectuals such as John Stuart Mill, the German philosopher G.W. Hegel and latterly Karl Marx were convinced of the static nature of the Subcontinent's history, as if it had frozen in time since the Vedic period. As Edward Said (1995) says, it was 'a way of coming to terms with the Orient that is based on the Orient's special place in European Western experience,' as a cultural 'other' to be dominated by the West. Or in Marx's reasoning, it could not rule itself, so it had to be ruled.

The economies of the colonised countries were adjusted to serve imperial needs. The demand for cash crops distorted agricultural systems, damaged the land and drove up market prices for native produce. Native industries which were potential rivals to British industry, such as the manufacture of cotton cloth, were subjected to crippling duties or even actively destroyed. Feudal land ownership along hereditary lines was introduced to serve imperial needs. This system had a particularly detrimental effect on women, who could no longer sow crops on land which was no longer communal. The British, in 1793, turned the old *Zamindar*, the tax collectors, into landowners with the power to evict peasants for not paying the revenue required of them. The tax was a flat rate which, unlike the previous arrangements, took no account of the conditions which affect yield, such as drought or floods. The ruined former employees provided cheap labour for cash crop plantations at home and abroad. Women's position in industries such as cotton, silk, jewellery, iron, pottery, glass and paper declined. The industries of cotton, muslin and world-famous brocade for the aristocracy, which India had produced for centuries, and in which women had played a significant part in spinning and weaving, were devastated by competition from British products and crippling taxation.

The role of the education systems in colonised countries was to produce armies of low-grade clerks and servants needed by the imperial machine; the colonised were discouraged from acquiring an education which could cause discontent with their status. Women were further excluded from holding high governmental positions, as training was often given in Britain. Such imperial policies destroyed self-confidence and impoverished the intellectual climate, as well as creating real poverty. The liberal religious and intellectual tradition sustained since the time of the great Mogul Emperor Akbar in the sixteenth century was lost.

For their own purposes the British produced a small elite of English-speaking Indians educated in the Western style of thinking and dress, with every incentive to identify with their imperial masters and distance themselves from their less well-educated compatriots. The 1851 War of Independence, led by the *nawabs*, showed that direct annexation of states was too costly. Thereafter the Empire created a few puppet state *rajas* and even *rani*, who would serve it, collect its taxes, and act as buffers between imperial interests and mass movements of national liberation. Western-style education was an important tool in this. The largely powerless principalities (some headed by women) were allowed to exist, but the seeds of religious suspicion and hatred were sown in their soil. Prior to British rule it was common for Muslim rulers to employ Hindus or Sikhs in the highest ranks within their states, and vice versa. The conflict between states had been on political and not religious grounds. Sometimes the wars had Hindu soldiers fighting for a Muslim ruler against another Hindu state, and vice versa (Dutt, 1949). Particular groupings like Brahmins or Sayyads held firmly to their newly-privileged position under the Raj, while using their knowledge within their respective religions to increase orthodoxy and rigidity.

The British also played a large part in the spread of Indian peoples around the world. After the abolition of slavery in 1833 in Britain, a system of indentured labour was instituted, whereby local populations were transported to different parts of the British Empire, for example to Mauritius, the West Indies and South America to grow sugar cane, in Southern Africa to first build and then work on the railways, and in East Africa to perform administrative tasks (Wolpert, *ibid*). Some Indian men married into the local populations of their new-found homes; others followed the well-trodden path of bringing wives from the country of origin. Women in these situations continued to be at a disadvantage. As is usual in situations of economic migration, men leave first to secure employment before being joined by either existing or future family units. They are exposed to the cultures and language of the new country immediately – through demands of work – channels not always open to women doing their isolated domestic duties.

## The effect on women and their roles during British colonial rule

Women lost heavily under these social and political changes, being generally excluded from education and losing their inheritance rights. They were also subjected to the increasingly reactionary religious and cultural forces created as a response to imperialism and used by the colonisers to sustain it. The institutions of purdah, which affected all native communities, and of sati, mainly affecting Hindus, were promoted. In the case of Hindu women, the concept of *karma* (fate) was used to suppress potential revolt. For the colonialists, the separation of male workers from their potential dependants, either by isolating women through purdah or eliminating them through sati, increased the men's availability as a transportable cheap labour force. Even though those who worked in the coal mines, cotton and wool industries, and tea plantations were ill-treated and badly paid, they still bore the burden of heavy taxation (Johnson and Sin, *Exploitation in India,* quoted in Dutt, *ibid*).Women were exploited most of all.

Some of the most fundamental rights of Muslim women were taken from them under colonial rule. Muslim women who had had the right to inherit property and wealth in their own right and keep their earned income were particularly affected. Their rights were brought into line with those of Hindu women, who could only 'safe-keep' the land for their minor sons, and whose only 'inheritance' came in the form of dowry upon her marriage – and which was handed to her husband's family. The fact that British women, who could not own property in their own right until 1870 is often omitted by British historians. As Maila Stevens (1975), writing about women's land rights in Malaysia, records:

> In South East Asia, European administrations have transferred rights in land from women to men ... The British administration took the first step in the change favourable to men when it was decided that only the land which was under actual cultivation would continue to pass in the female line, whereas the areas serving as fallow land in shifting cultivation had to be registered to ensure the continuance of female inheritance. In this way, the women lost their rights to forest land ...

The increase of sati in Bengal provides an interesting insight into how the most reactionary religious elements joined forces with British colonialism to undermine women. The state of Bengal, by virtue of its great prosperity, had a significant number of wealthy families. Hindu women, although owning no property in their own right, benefited from the general position of their families. Widows could 'safe-keep' the family state for their minor sons until they were old enough to inherit the land. By the pundits insisting that sati was an integral part of Hinduism and that a Hindu woman could show her devotion to her deceased husband and prove her purity by entering into self-immolation, they would free the family property which could then be incorporated into the British state.

After 1857, when the national uprising against British rule (the so-called 'Indian Mutiny') was defeated, Muslim and Hindu women's struggle against the British colonial rule became tied up with reinstatement of their rights under Islam and Hinduism respectively. The rights of Muslims as a separate religious group had become submerged under colonial rule. The reassertion of their identity by Muslim women was part of the struggle for independence.

During the nineteenth century women's rights and legal status were supported by male social reformers like Rammohun Roy and Seyyed Ahmad Khan. Women and men engaged in the struggle were influenced not only by their exposure to international events like the French Revolution and the American War of Independence in the previous century but also by the rediscovery of ancient India and its learning.

> It was as the consolidation of British power during the nineteenth century which eroded the position of women; changes in property laws in favour of men were to the disadvantage of the matrilineal societies of south India. The destruction of the home-based small industries forced women into appalling conditions in factories, and the new taxes on property forced both men and women into paid labour to meet these new demands. (Visram, 1992).

15

Indeed, the position of women in the Subcontinent so deteriorated that young girls of poor families who could not pay their taxes were sold off. Many ended in licensed brothels for the use of British soldiers, contracted venereal diseases as a result of their slavery, and were abandoned both by their families and their owners once their usefulness was over.

## The struggle for independence

Throughout the eighteenth and nineteenth centuries people in different social groupings found their interests curtailed. The aristocracy were stripped of their political powers, the industrialists found themselves squeezed by British industries, the landlords found themselves serving the interests of imperial powers, and the working-classes became increasingly stateless, bearing the heaviest burden of exploitation. International movements, from the American War of Independence to the Russian Revolutions of 1905 and 1917, influenced different sections of society in different ways. The impact of these nationalist ideals upon economic hardship united the various interest groups. Upper- and middle-class women came out of their purdah and *zanana* and acted as role models for working-class women so that the movement could have a mass appeal.

Women began to challenge colonial rule and to be actively involved in the movement to gain independence. They used their own space in the *zanana* or they dispensed with purdah altogether, as the occasion demanded, to participate in the struggle for independence. Their own men encouraged them to leave the confines of *zanana* to participate actively. For some men the liberation of their women lay in the discarding of gender boundaries. In 1889, ten women, mostly from Bombay and Calcutta, attended the fourth session of the Indian National Congress. Many middle-class women had begun to take an interest in politics by the end of the century; the partition of Bengal in 1905 led many women into active campaigning. It was then that the *swadeshi* movement, to buy and wear only home-produced goods, began. Women were significantly involved; a British journalist wrote in 1910:

> The revolt seems to have obtained a firm hold in the *zanana* (women's quarters) and the Hindu woman behind the purdah often exercises a greater influence on her husband and sons than the English women who move so freely about the world...' (Valentine Chirol, 1910, quoted in Visram, *ibid.*).

Bengal, the province of legendary wealth and intellectual heritage, was at the forefront of the liberation movement. This posed a threat to the British authorities. Lord Curzon, the Viceroy, partitioned Bengal in 1905 for the ostensible reason that it was too big to govern as one state. The liberation movement's petition against this move was greeted by the British authorities with silence, so Indians decided to take direct action by boycotting foreign goods, using only home-grown materials. This tactic was also successfully used in Egypt by women in their struggle to gain independence from British colonial rule, and had an earlier model in the Boston Tea Party. The process of partition in 1947 cut in half the two most prosperous provinces of British India, Bengal and Punjab.

The First World War was a watershed. Not only did many of the 1.3 million men contributed by India to the army fail to return, leaving their women to head their households alone, but many women also were involved in the war effort. In 1914, 16,000 British and 28,500 Indian troops left Karachi bound for Marseilles, leading the American *New York World* newspaper to comment that: 'Its 'native' contingent belongs to a civilisation that was old when Germany was a forest, and early Britons stained their naked bodies blue' (Wolpert, 1989). After the war, the political reforms promised by the British failed to materialise, leading to increased civil strife. Men and women together organised political meetings. One at Amritsar in 1919 resulted in a massacre by the British under General Dyer. The meeting was in fact to celebrate a Hindu festival, but the British could take no chances. Struggle continued, culminating in the independence of India and its partition in 1947.

The differential treatment meted out to Muslims and Hindus was crystallised at the time of partition in 1947, when the new country of Pakistan was formed as two widely separated halves with over a thousand miles of Indian territory between them, and with very little in common except religion. Their languages are mutually incomprehensible, and there is no common script. Most of the provinces of what is now Pakistan were the divided portions of the former states of Punjab, Kashmir and Sindh. Former princely states such as Hyderabad lost their sovereignty and became part of India, despite their Muslim majority and Muslim rulers. Partition had devastating social and economic implications. Many people died, families were divided and large cities like Calcutta lost the agricultural hinterland which had supplied the raw materials for their factories and, whose goods were shipped through their ports and railways. The canal system watering the fertile Indus valley was arbitrarily divided, causing economic problems to this day. The complications of water supply along the Ganges and Brahmaputra involve the separate countries of India, Nepal and Bangladesh.

One of the major reasons for the considerable participation of women in the independence struggle was the absence of so many of their men, imprisoned by the British. Jawaharlal Nehru, Prime Minister of India from 1947 to 1964 and a Congress leader during the height of the struggle, paid tribute to women's contributions and the risks they took in the national liberation movement. Women across the social divide left their former positions to join hands in a mass movement. Even government orders and police batons did not deter them.

Most of the menfolk were in prison. And then a remarkable thing happened. Our women came to the front and took charge of the struggle. Women had always been there, of course, but now there was an avalanche of them, which took not only the British government but their own menfolk by surprise. Here were these women, women of the upper or middle-classes, leading sheltered lives in their homes, peasant women, working-class women, rich women, poor women, pouring out in their tens of thousands in defiance of government order and police *lathi*....(Nehru, 1989).

Women continued to make their presence felt on the domestic as well as the international scene. In 1930 they attended a Round Table conference in London to discuss Indian aspirations for self-government. One of their demands was for the vote; Begum Jahannara Shah Nawaz wrote:

We decided to ask for adult suffrage, but if that was not possible, to frame qualifications for franchise in such a manner that women should become a substantial portion of the electorate and should be given an effective voting strength. More, we asked for reserved seats for women in all the legislatures for only two elections (Jahannara Shah Nawaz, quoted in Visram, 1993).

What is striking in the history of this area is both the continuity of the culture and its ability to absorb outside influences. Every invasion or immigration has left a cultural, religious, racial or linguistic mark on the Indian Subcontinent, which has shown an infinite capacity to absorb and subsume all these influences. There has also been response to the influences of the transported populations, some of whom have now found their way back home, and some who have stayed in their new lands while keeping contact with their original homes.

## A pattern of complexity: some aspects of modern Indian Subcontinent culture

The cultures of the Subcontinent have been dominated, in both myth and reality, by the village. There are over one million villages, but not all are the small, sleepy and remote hamlets conjured up by the word 'village'. Some villages are comparable in size to a small British town. Villages on the Subcontinent have their own hierarchy of class, income, culture and occupation; the regulation of village life is usually conducted by the *panchayat*, the open court system of village elders, governing most aspects of day-to-day life. One aspect of village life which has passed from the village is the control of the registration of land by the local land registrar, or *patwari*. All land ownership is now on a computerised record, which simplifies greatly the organisation of tax liability, inheritance and tenants' rights. Villages also vary in their relationship with the outside world; some are, indeed, exceedingly remote, while others are beginning to resemble the British 'dormitory town'. The advent of satellite television, now covering the whole of the Subcontinent, has led to an explosion of television ownership.

Many towns and cities of the Subcontinent are long established. For example, Delhi not only boasts the famous Red Fort but also the '*Purana Qulah*' (Old Fort) now mostly ruined, within which is a Greek-style amphitheatre. In the Red Fort itself, there are private apartments for women, the *Rang Mahel*, the 'Palace of Colours', so called because of the dazzling decorative beauty of the crystal wall embellishments. The ceiling of the *Diwan-i-Khas*, or Hall of Private Audience, was opulently overlaid with gold and almost entirely covered by raised gold and silver foliage, studded with precious stones. A French traveller some time after 1820 estimated the value as at 27 million francs. It is now a shadow of its former self, due to neglect and looting during the colonial period.

Links with the rest of the world have always been extensive. The Subcontinent, subject to invasions and immigration, and involved in trade over most of the known world, has absorbed, transmuted and returned cultural influences from China, central Asia, the Near and Middle East, Europe – especially Islamic Spain – Africa and the Pacific basin. Notable donations to the world have included the almost universal present system of numbering, which the Arabs transmitted to the rest of the world, and the addition of sugar, from the sugar-cane, to our diet – but not the chilli.

What is remarkable about the influence of the Subcontinent today is the total penetration of film culture. The vast empire of Bollywood, besides creating its own version of Hindi to increase intelligibility to the widest variety of audiences on the Subcontinent, has now penetrated television and thereby the video market. Its influence extends far beyond the Subcontinent (Gokalsingh and Dessanyake, 1998). Almost every Asian corner store in Britain vibrates to the sound of *filmi* songs. 'Curry' cuisine has reached towns and cities in Europe, including Paris, after the cautious beginnings under the British Raj which created Mulligatawny soup, a translation of a south Indian pepper water dish to something more suited to the *Sahib*'s table. The 'Indian' cooking commercially available in Europe and North America fails to do justice to the subtle and complex range of cuisines available on the Subcontinent. There are considerable differences between the meat-based, rich sauces of the Moghul cooking of Northwest India, the fish- and rice-based dishes of Bengal, the vegetarian food of Gujerat and the fiery spices of Madras, to name only a few.

Styles of housing vary even more than cuisine. Responses to climatic variation ensure that there is little similarity between, for example, the mostly flat-roofed houses of Karachi, the largest city in Pakistan, and the pitched roofs of the buildings in the Kailash valley in the Himalayan foothills, also in Pakistan. Some houses, for example in Bengal in India, traditionally incorporate large, shuttered windows and wide doors to ensure maximum breeziness in the oppressive summer heat. Often houses are built around a courtyard, used as a central working area; in some cases the house is divided into two parts, with a public reception area and another area for domestic privacy. The size, shape and even the materials from which the house is made may reflect these geographical and climatic variations, as do the age of the building, the socio-economic position and the caste and religious traditions of the present or former inhabitants.

The clothes that women wear also reflect in a complex manner this variety of influences. The Moghul empire and the coming of Islam brought the scarf to cover the head, the baggy trousers and the long-sleeved tunic to Northwest and Central India becoming today's *dupatta, shalwar* and *qumeez*. Moghul courtly dress included the *gharara*, extremely flared trousers, gathered at the knees, with a short tight *qumeez* and very long *dupatta*, worn even now for ceremonial occasions such as weddings. The *sari* is a relatively recent development; ancient Indian dress consisted of a long flared skirt, with a separate wide scarf, draped over the upper half of the body. Sometimes, but not always, this was accompanied by a short-sleeved tight blouse which did not cover the midriff. This style, always including a blouse, sometimes remarkably skimpy, is still worn in Gujerat, Rajastan and Sindh; indeed it is now high fashion and can be seen on the streets of London or Leicester. South Indian women may wear a sari of seven to nine yards long, and in the extreme south a separate skirt and a scarf draped over a blouse are still worn. Fashion, again, has blurred the geographical range of various clothing styles; the ease and convenience of the *shalwar qumeez* and *dupatta* makes this the clothing of choice for many fashionable young women across the Subcontinent. Traditional sari styles are almost infinitely variable, but modern young women may choose to adopt any style of dress currently in fashion, drawn from any tradition, including those of Europe. Indeed the fashion styles of Bombay or Karachi can vie with those of Paris or Rome.

Music and dance are equally complex in tradition and antiquity, but living and breathing in a way that has disappeared from Western Europe. In song, the classical Hindu tradition of *ragas*, whose roots can be traced back at least two thousand years, and the Muslim traditions of *ghazal* and *quwaali* are often transmitted orally as well as in written form; the oral tradition is highly developed and respected on a par with the written word. The equally ancient *bharat natyam* or *odissi* dance styles, and the *kathak* style of dance patronised by the Moghul courts, are still widely practised. Folk dances and songs still form an important part of life, although nowadays popular culture depends heavily on films and television.

There exists today a vast body of classical Hindu religious texts, as well as scientific, mathematical, astrological, philosophical and poetic works. The other religious communities have their own literatures; the Sikhs pay great respect to the book of their traditions in every *Gurdwara*. The polymath Rabindranath Tagore from Bengal was awarded the Nobel prize for literature early in the twentieth century. In addition to high literature, there is popular culture in English and the many languages of the Subcontinent, including some splendid comics and children's literature.

The oral tradition of learning is long and well developed. Teachers transmitted traditions to pupils over thousands of years before any written text existed. This tradition still exists in the Muslim world, and to some extent in Judaism, where young people are encouraged to commit to memory the whole of their scriptures. The advantage of this method was that even in troubled times, when books could be destroyed, the learning remained in the memories of scholars. During the British Raj, when the education system severely limited educational opportunities for women, the oral tradition was all-important. Women could pass down to posterity the knowledge and experiences of their people.

This vital oral tradition, especially among women, is largely ignored and devalued in Britain, where women without literacy skills are dismissed as ignorant and not worth listening to. The phrase 'They are not even literate in their own language' implies: 'What can you expect of them?' and 'How can we, as professionals, be expected to teach them?' The most patronising attitudes displayed towards the Asian community in general and women in particular are from the very professionals who earn their livelihood through being employed to work with them, for example school teachers, youth and community workers, social workers, teachers of English as an additional language and medical professionals. This attitude is reminiscent of the destruction of the Roman baths and drains by the Anglo-Saxon invaders to Britain because they had no idea what they were for. The complexities of Asian women are summed up in one dismissive phrase: 'ethnic minority'.

# Chapter 3

# Ethnic minority women: their religious roles and expectations

Shumma in sati
The veil tells the tale
'Whose lost love?' ask the mirrors
Bhunvra in sajood is the true picture
Strings of pearls fall from her eyes
Kissing her cheeks, there they lie

The phrases 'ethnic minority women', 'their religions', 'their roles and expectations' are glibly bandied about in Western academic and government circles. The term 'ethnic minority women' is used interchangeably with 'Asians' to describe women from the Subcontinent, so epitomising the whole notion of 'otherness'. Encapsulated within 'ethnic minority' is a host of assumptions about the 'otherness' of Asian women. They are different from 'us', the white researchers and professionals, and their religious roles and expectations are at variance with ours. 'We' know who 'we' are, and these others, whom we term ethnic minorities, are here to be studied. 'We' can be religious, secular, agnostic or atheist; but ethnic minority women can only be religious, for that is an inherent part of their culture and their being.

The assumption is that 'we' are white Westerners, who by a quirk of history live where we do. 'Our' country happens to be Christian, although that does not impinge on our consciousness or our daily lives. We are rational, intelligent people who make our own decisions according to a set of circumstances and we may or may not have a nodding acquaintance with a religion. The others of a 'darker, inferior' race are not endowed with the same degree of rational thought and liberal tolerance, and are governed by the whims of fundamentalist *mullahs* or ignorant sectarian priests: they veil their women, have them hidden away from public life.

*The Bride –    East ...    and West*

They have their marriages arranged, allowing them no freedom, and eventually they may even be burnt to death at their husbands' funeral pyres.

Throughout the nineteenth and twentieth centuries there has been both fascination with and repulsion towards the institutions of purdah (female veiling and seclusion, one aspect of which is known as *hareem* or *zanana*) and sati, the burning alive of a widow on the funeral pyre of her deceased husband. These institutions symbolise the East, the Indian Subcontinent and are associated with Islam and Hinduism respectively. The Orient was and is ever constant, never changing, to be studied by the West through rational, analytical eyes. Both traditions may be viewed within the context of white European colonialism/neo-colonialism and also against the backdrop of patriarchal and patrilineal societies.

The reality of purdah and how it affects the daily lives of women in the Subcontinent requires examination. Purdah is investigated in four different contexts: historical, religious, societal and economic. Notions surrounding purdah are also examined: that it exists to keep women submissive; that it serves to exclude women from paid work; and finally that women do not struggle against the confines of their lives. It seems to me that purdah is seen by most Westerners as almost a prerequisite of Islam, designed to keep women in their place, which they accept without question. This chapter also touches upon arranged marriages, divorce, and fundamentalism; and it indicates that women across religious, socio-economic and political boundaries share a common experience: second-class status.

The compartmentalisation of women into 'ethnic minority women' and others prevents serious debate on the position of women as second-class citizens in modern societies. This book shows how Asian women in Britain find that their rights as individuals, to marriage, education or career, are under constant attack because of the way they are stereotyped.

The term 'ethnic minority', usually applied as a euphemism with a connotation of inferiority, is ill-defined. 'Ethnic minority women', used even more loosely, is even less well-defined. According to Collins' dictionary, the term *ethnic* relates to a human group having racial, religious, linguistic or certain other traits in common; also to classification of mankind into groups, on the basis of racial characteristics. By either definition, there are several different 'ethnic minorities' among the peoples originally from the Subcontinent.

Just as a white Western woman could be a Jain, Hindu, Muslim, Sikh, Jewish, Christian or Parsi, an Indian woman could be Christian, Buddhist or Muslim. The roles and expectations of women within each of the religions would depend upon her socio-economic position and where and when she lived rather than upon the religious doctrine *per se*. Nor can the practice of a religion be totally separated from the culture within which it is located. For instance, Islam in Java is very different from Islam in France or Saudi Arabia. The practice of a religion is as different as the societies in which it flourishes. Local customs are often incorporated into religious rites and life is lived and observed by on-lookers as well as believers as if they were inseparable from the scriptures: the divine message – a religious imperative. This applies to both sati and purdah. They are no more central to Hinduism or Islam than Father Christmas is to the Christain faith. Furthermore, religious practices change and evolve as do other social institutions – take  for example the ordination of women by the Church of England in 1992.

## The white man's burden

Western intellectuals, including radicals such as Karl Marx, were convinced that colonised peoples were incapable of self-government. 'They cannot represent themselves; they must be represented' (Marx, quoted in Said, 1995). The 'white man's burden' stressed the role of civilising the natives, who were perceived to be barbaric, over-sexed and unruly. White women too played a role in holding up the colonial edifice and oiling its apparatus, as illustrated in a novel by Mrs. General Mainwaring published in 1830, *The Suttee, or Hindoo Converts*.

> It is painful to reflect that whilst Britain has made vast exertions to establish a mighty empire in the East, little has been done to emancipate the Hindoos from the bondage of superstition, under which they have been so long kept the sanguinary priesthood. At length the call for philanthropy is raised, and the abominations which defile British India must be exterminated. When that desirable work is accomplished, then may it be expected, that the mild quiescent morality of the Hindoo character will bring forth fruits of righteousness, by the influence of the Gospel.

The novel is set in the southern India of Tipu Sultan, who presented a formidable threat to Britain's expansionist policies and consequently was demonised as an 'oriental despot'. Temora, the heroine, is a virtuous wife of a Hindu prince who dies in battle, whereupon she is forced by the wicked Brahmin Benrudda to enter her husband's funeral pyre. Temora is rescued by British soldiers and saved by converting to Christianity. Benrudda is shot dead and falls into the funeral pyre intended for Temora (Lewis in Hawley, 1994). Sati, like purdah, became a symbol for the East which was tantalising, compelling and terrifyingly repulsive. Its excesses had to be moderated by the helping hand of the white man and the true religion, Christianity.

## Purdah

Purdah has captured the imagination of poets, artists and travellers. It has evoked much literature and continues to be a subject of debate both within and without the cultures with which it is associated. Television advertising in Britain has added to the plethora of associations. In a recent advertisement, the caption *Full of Eastern promise* accompanies images of a bejewelled scantily dressed woman, with the body of a contortionist, in a harem offering Turkish or some other kind of delight. At the other end of the spectrum we find Urdu poets referring to someone's beloved in purdah whose attraction is thus made all the greater by this unattainability; or some legendary *purdah nasheen*, so pure and secluded that even the moon and stars yearn for glimpses of her. Her alabaster body and dazzling beauty, the envy of the moon queen herself, is cocooned in a web of purdah from the harsh rays of the sun or the common gaze of mere mortals. Her character unblemished, her beauty untarnished, she is such stuff as a man's dreams are made of. Purdah can be an excuse for debarring women from full socio-economic and political life, controlling women's space and movement, to ensure pre-marital chastity and post-marital fidelity. Alternatively it can be seen as a 'safe' area in which women can relax, be creative and supportive, henna their hands, oil their hair, have their bodies massaged, plot against their men – especially their husbands – earn and spend income, and organise socio-political revolution. Literary and historical evidence both point to all these uses that purdah has been put to. It has been used as a symbol of liberation and as religious obscurantism.

*Harem* comes from the Arabic word *haram* meaning forbidden. In other words it was a space for women which was *haram* or out of bounds for all men except the woman's husband or blood relatives with whom marriage is disallowed, for example father or paternal uncles. All men with whom marriage could be contracted, including first cousins, would, strictly speaking, be forbidden to enter the harem. *Harem* is simply the women's quarters or area; in practice, the concept may include polygyny, monogamy, concubines, or nuclear families. Once the concept of *haram* is defined, women carry it with them to ensure their behaviour accords with their social standing. This all-embracing notion of *harem* can be puzzling to outsiders and even to some within the culture, especially children.

Fathima Mernissi, in her book *The Harem Within: Tales of a Moroccan Girlhood* (1995), describes a childhood debate between her and her young cousins about what constitutes harem. Is harem a place where a man lives with many women, or is it separate living quarters for women? Only when her grandmother explained that the word harem is derived from '*haram*', and that 'once you knew what was forbidden, you carried the harem within', could she begin to make some sense of the observed complexities of the different degrees of seclusion.

## What is purdah?

*Purdah* is a Farsi word meaning curtain. The curtain can be literal or metaphorical. It can be the division between the two worlds of men and women. The division which the curtain represents is between unequals, with the smaller part designated for women. It exists in various forms and levels: psychological, social, physical and organisational. It defines for women their space, mode of behaviour and the thinking which underpins the tradition. The psychological aspect is perhaps the most significant. When women venture outside the space assigned to them and into the men's arena, they do so on terms defined for them by men, which are supported through an intricate web of social behaviours for both men and women. Even when there are no practical means of practising purdah, for example through a harem or even *burqua*, women carry with them the constraints of it in their psyche and this manifests itself in their behaviour. The purpose of purdah is to ensure the sexual 'purity' of women who are perceived to be 'respectable' and who would be responsible for producing sons to inherit the property and wealth of a patriarch. The observation of purdah, therefore, is stricter among the upper classes. There have always been women for whom purdah was deemed unnecessary. But some women who are regarded as disreputable may wear *burqua* as a mask to camouflage their identity and allow themselves the freedom of movement in the streets they would not otherwise enjoy.

> The institution of purdah is the linchpin of a complex system of arrangements to ensure the pre-marital chastity and post-marital fidelity of women ... Purdah also operates at an ideological level: It prescribes the correct mode of behaviour for women, enjoining them to be modest and submissive, and endows them with the status of a vulnerable and protected group (Kabeer, 1984).

As property and other inheritance was, and largely still is, along patrilineal lines (Kabeer *op. cit.,* Kelsey, 1991) the authenticity of the inheritor is of paramount importance. So adultery by a wife could be tantamount to treason. Henry VIII had Anne Boleyn beheaded because he suspected her of adultery. Purdah is a way of ensuring post-marital chastity, thus upholding patriarchy.

> Purdah originally evolved as a means of controlling women in the dominant feudal or tribal group (Shaheed and Mumtaz, 1987).

Other groups have tried to emulate purdah, but it only works for those able to forego female labour. This does not detract from its importance for women who could not practise full purdah for financial reasons, for they continue to try to emulate their wealthier counterparts. Consequently, a veiled woman has become a symbol of social status, proclaiming that: 'I am so rich that my wife doesn't have to work'. As Mernissi, (1986) observes: 'A family's financial position to support its women so that they do not have to work is closely intertwined with the whole concept of purdah'.

Under the Umayyad Caliph Walid II (tenth century AD) the Arab ruling class enjoyed unprecedented opulence. With this came licentious pleasures, and dancing girls flooded to Baghdad. It was to separate the respectable women from the dancing girls that purdah arose, and seclusion of females was practised in ancient imperial Iran. As the democratically elected caliph increasingly acted as a hereditary monarch, more of the Iranian royal customs were adopted.

## The origins of purdah

In Plato's Greece well-bred women lived in seclusion in their familial or marital homes (Loomis, 1942). This was also the tradition in the Persian empire and parts of northern India before the Moghuls (Altekar, 1973). In Syria and Egypt in 500-323 BC free women were, according to Sarah Pomeroy:

> ...usually secluded so that they could not be seen by men who were not close relatives. An orator could maintain that some women were even too modest to be seen by men who were relatives, and for a strange man to intrude upon free women in the house of another man was tantamount to a criminal act (Pomeroy quoted in L. Ahmed, 1992).

Female seclusion was well established in Iran and the Eastern Mediterranean areas conquered by Islam from the eighth century AD. In Mesopotamia between 3500 and 3000 BC large urban centres developed which had a war culture which favoured men and became land ownership inherited through the male line. Women, through whom the production of inheritors was secured, became the first property to be owned, firstly by the father and then by the husband. This was institutionalised and sanctioned by the state. A woman's body and her sexuality became something to be negotiated between men, in particular father and husband. Her premarital chastity and post-marital fidelity had to be ensured if male inheritance laws were to be effective. The Assyrian state actually legislated for the protocol on veiling. Gerder Lerner, quoted in Ahmed (1992) provides an illuminating insight into this arrangement. Wives and daughters of feudal lords or 'seignors' were compelled to veil, as were the concubines who accompanied their mistresses and 'sacred prostitutes' who were subsequently married, whereas slaves and harlots were forbidden to veil. Purdah or veiling was therefore not only a mark of social distinction; it separated out women who were protected from those who were sexually available. Anyone veiling illegally was severely punished – her tongue was cut out. The Jewish Talmud, from AD 600 onwards, allowed a man to divorce a wife who appeared in public with her head uncovered, whilst St Paul went as far as to say that if a woman prayed bareheaded she should have her head shaved (I Corinthians II, VI).

Altekar's account (1973) shows that the earliest reference to purdah in India is c.100 BC. It refers to the royal women who practised it to protect themselves from the vulgar gaze. The *Rāmāyana*, referring to Sita embarking on a journey to Ayodhya, observes that: 'a lady, who had so far not been seen even by the spirits of the sky, should now become the object of public gaze.' And a similar observation is made in the *Mahabharata* about Dhritarashtra's departing to the forest. In the dramatist Bhasa's (c.200 AD) *Pratima*, Sita is depicted in a veil, although Rama asks her to unveil. The *Dhammāpada* (c.300 AD) refers to women travelling in covered carriages and marriageable maidens being segregated and not allowed to be served by male servants. This is reminiscent of the Turkish harem system in which women were served by other women or eunuchs, a system which prevailed until the collapse of the Ottoman Empire after the First World War.

In the drama of *Mrichchhakdtika* the countess Vasantsena is offered a veil when she is raised to the status of a respectable lady. There are also references made to *anatahpuram* (inner quarters) and *avaradha* (a place inaccessible) – presumably to strange men if her husband was away.

Altekar is at pains to demonstrate that the reference to purdah applied to Sita in the Ramayana was a later interpolation and that the practice was confined to a small geographical area in Northern India amongst a few women of royal blood, which became more widespread during the Christian and latterly Islamic eras. She does, however, concede that '... we find that even in pre-Muslim times there was a section of society from c.100 BC which advocated the use of the veil for royal ladies for the purposes of increasing prestige' (Altekar, 1973).

The point is that purdah indisputably pre-dates Islam and was practised by upper-class Greeks, Indians and Persian women before Islam (Altekar *ibid.*, Kabeer *op. cit.*). Purdah was never applied to all women across the social boundaries; it depended upon the social standing of the woman (usually of royal blood) and served as a mark of social distinction. Repeated reference to veiling or seclusion imply that the woman behind the barrier is chaste. Veiling of the bride appears to be a common thread in many Western and Eastern cultures, perhaps signifying that a bride sold by her father had her veil lifted by the husband only after the contract was signed. One of the earliest recorded references to the tradition of veiling from the future husband is in the Old Testament: Rebecca, who had been freely conversing with the servant, veils herself before meeting her prospective husband:

> ... she had said unto the servant, What man is this that walketh the field to meet us? And the servant had said, it is my master: therefore she took her veil and covered herself. (Genesis 24, lxv)

After the marriage a woman lost her identity by taking on her husband's name (Pomeroy, 1976). In most Western cultures this is still the norm. Both the veiling and taking the husband's name feeds male sexual fantasy and ascribes a correct mode of behaviour for the woman, worthy of male respect. As in all social interactions female acquiescence is needed, which is usually gained by engendering a feeling of specialness and social prestige, internalised by women who adopt the practice.

As we have seen, female seclusion was established practice long before Islam and, along with other local customs, was incorporated into the religion as it spread through different parts of the world. The verse in the Quran which refers to the seclusion of women can be translated as:

> And when you ask his wives for anything, ask it of them from behind a curtain (*hejjab*). That is purer for your hearts and their hearts.

This revelation arose during the Prophet's controversial marriage to Zeinab, the former wife of Zaid, whom he had adopted and raised as a son. This practice of seclusion was exclusive to the Prophet's wives from that time, and was not then of general application. Taking the veil in fact became synonymous with being the Prophet's wife. His wife Ayesha, who had until then circulated freely among men, found the practice restrictive. Twenty-four years after Muhammad's death, she went to war against Ali, husband of Fatima, the daughter of the Prophet. She was supporting the right of Ottoman to succeed to the caliphate after the death of Omar, the second caliph, who had pressed to extend the seclusion of women beyond the Prophet's wives. After Ottoman was murdered, Ayesha was disastrously defeated by Ali's armies. It was not until one hundred and fifty years after Prophet Muhammad's death that the practice of female seclusion became widespread. Then purdah spread from Arabia to other areas that had by then become Islamic. It coincided with the expansion of Islam to places in which upper-class women were veiled.

Naila Kabeer (1984 *ibid*) notes that:

> Although purdah is generally identified with Islam, it should be emphasised that various forms of female seclusion are practised all over the Indian Subcontinent by both Muslim and Hindu families. The practice of purdah often represents the social status of the family rather than its religious persuasion.

Women's submission was due not to Islamic ideas but to secular constraints which did not disappear when Islamic teaching attained widespread influence. In the Qazi Court, the highest authority of Islamic jurisprudence in Pakistan, the federal Shariat court has held that there was no justification for purdah either in Quran or Sunnah (Islamic tradition).

## The colonial legacy

Western perceptions during colonial and post-colonial periods have woven a web of contradictory images around the notion of female seclusion. Because of the ways in which our concepts are culturally constructed, in certain cases over a long period of imperial domination, mention of the term *harem* instantaneously conjures up dual images of a rather scantily dressed belly dancer and a woman clad in an all-enveloping gown. Both are of course Muslim women, as the institution is associated solely with Islam, and the helpless victims who accept their lot without question. This construct of foreign women is part of an ideology about the East which supported the imperialist projects of European states. Comparison with historical fact, widely documented, will show how false, oversimplified ideas not only supported the 'inferiority' of colonised nations but, by obscuring similarities between the oppressed and the oppressor, reinforced a spurious sense of superiority in the colonisers.

Some of the more fanciful descriptions of the delights or oppressions of the harem produced during the eighteenth and nineteenth centuries were written by men who could never enter it. Accounts by European women, such as Lady Montague or Mary Eliza Rogers, based on their own observations, were somehow undervalued in the canon of 'harem literature'. Lady Montague, a Turkophile, in her letter to Lady Margaret extols the virtue of wearing the *yashmak* because it affords the wearer a degree of anonymity and therefore freedom she would not otherwise have. This freedom is far greater than that enjoyed by women of the same class in the West at the time.

> It is very easy to see that they have more liberty than we have, no woman of that rank so ever being permitted to go into the streets without two Muslims, one that covers her face all but her eyes and another that hides the whole dress of her head. You may guess how effectively this disguises them... this perpetual masquerade gives them entire liberty of following their inclination without danger of discovery (Melman, 1995).

Lady Montague comments on Turkish women's freedom to own property and to keep their own income in marriage and after divorce, in addition to financial settlement from their husbands. This was in sharp contrast to the position of women in Europe at the time. The Married Women's Property Act in Britain which enabled married women to keep their own property instead of it becoming their husbands' was not passed until 1870. Mrs Craven, who was not a Turkophile, was impressed by the way in which a wife can indicate her need for privacy by putting a pair of slippers outside the door separating the *haremlik* from the *selemlik*. The use of yellow indoor slippers in this way acts as a metaphor for freedom. The right of a wife to refuse her husband's sexual demands was not won in Britain until the mid nineteen nineties.

Clearly purdah was neither confined to nor exclusively practised by Muslim women: nor is its practice uniformly applied throughout history. For example, upper-class Jewish, Christian and Muslim women alike lived in harems and were under purdah in Egypt in the early twentieth century (Shaarawi, 1986). Orthodox Jewish women still cover their hair or crop it and wear a wig. Ginzberg says that 'a woman covers her hair in token of Eve's having brought sin into the world; she tries to hide her shame; and women precede men in a funeral cortege, because it was a woman who brought death into the world'. (Ginsberg in Baring and Cash, 1991). Literary as well as factual references point to the existence of some form of female seclusion, albeit not universally applied to women across India or, indeed, being accepted without protest.

It is noteworthy that Katija, the Prophet Muhammad's first wife, was a business-woman in her own right and was not in purdah. She managed some of her business affairs herself and others through male employees. Indeed it was through her business relationship that she knew Muhammad who was later to receive prophet-hood and to whom she sent a message of marriage. His youngest wife Ayesha, through whom was transmitted the *Hadith* (the collected sayings of the Prophet), mingled freely with men and fought in battles. Muhammad authorised Ayesha, to give religious advice, in his absence, telling Muslims to 'take half your religion from this woman' (Brooks, 1995). The *Hadith* was compiled one hundred and fifty years after the death of the Prophet, and the compiler, Hanbal, created a two-tier system in so doing. The *Quvi*, the recognised, was attributed to a man, Abu Hurara; *Zaeef*, the 'weak' majority of the *Hadith*, was attributed to Ayesha. Of the original 2,210 *Hadith* which were attributed to Ayesha, all but 174 were dismissed by the ninth-century male scholars.

## Degrees of purdah

There are various degrees of purdah, depending on the social position of the family, the individual women's own aspirations and the prevailing socio-political context. The Emperor Akbar in India, for example, had a separate palace, Panch Mahal built for the women at Fatah-poor-Sikri, within the same grounds but away from the area of political activity. During the Turkish Empire women of the royal household had a separate harem, and their counterparts during the Umayyad Dynasty in Andalucia and the reign of Shah-Jahan in India had what is known as *zanana*, a part of the palace designated for women. According to Laila Ahmed (1992) purdah found 'architectural expression' during the first century AD. There are, however, earlier references to women in ancient Greece whose living quarters faced away from the main streets. Men and women lived separate lives; democracy in the Athenian state did not extend to women.

This model of *zanana* (*haremlik*) or the male equivalent, *merdana* (*selemlik*), was emulated by other strata of society to varying degrees. Those with the economic means achieved it by allotting separate sections of the house to each gender. In wealthy households this division was achieved by assigning the most public areas to men and the rest to women. For example, wealthy households in Bangladesh had bamboo groves and fruit trees surrounding the house and their women only wore a *burqah* when they went outside their village. The *burqah* can be a single garment shaped like a shuttle-cock, or it can be in two pieces: a cape-like upper part with chiffon pieces to cover the face and a lower part like a knee- to full-length gown. The veil could be drawn over the face or lifted, depending on the degree of purdah the women wanted.

However, down the social scale where this material separation was not possible, a purdah was used to indicate the demarcation line. In homes where even this was not possible, a scarf over the head seemed to suffice. Such women had no *burqah* and the only expedient of purdah they practised was that of covering the head with *sari-pullu* (the free end of the sari, used to drape the body or hide the head, according to local custom). But it is the custom for women of any religion in the Sub-continent to cover the hair as a sign of respect and respectability. Whether it be Benazir Bhutto, Indira Ghandi or Begum Khalida Zia, these female Prime Ministers are typically shown with their heads covered. Conversely, poorer women had no privacy and carried out domestic chores in full view of passers-by. If all else fails, lowering the eyes can be seen as a sufficient sign of purdah. middle-class women practice purdah to distinguish themselves from working-class women.

A study carried out in Lahore (Pakistan) revealed that upper-class women did not have to wear *burqua* in order to establish their *izzat* or honour. For them wearing *chadar,* a shawl, or a *duputta*, a long gauzy scarf, was sufficient. Upper-class women did not wear *burqua* and lower-class women found it impractical when they conducted business transactions in the bazaar. This shift in attitudes was caused by upper-class women dispensing with purdah to take part in the struggle for independence against the British. However, as Donnan and Webner (1991) note:

> higher and lower status groups associate the wearing of burqua with people who are attempting to increase their position. All informants associated it with a conservative attitude, the expression of purdah (seclusion). The wearing of burqua is a sign of izzat.

Purdah, then, is subject to fashion.

It is curious how only upper-class women, who did not depend upon their earnings, could afford to be vulnerable ladies in the West and in purdah in the East. Working-class women had no such choice. They worked in the fields, building construction, down the mines or at other forms of labour appropriate to their station in life. For them the practical reality of earning a living takes precedence over any notion of symbolic class position. However, they could wear *burqah* to accord themselves a status they would not otherwise have.

The middle-classes which could not afford female economic inactivity compromised by having their women work in professions with separate female hierarchies such as teaching and medicine, two of the traditional female domains.

They could work in privacy in an all-women environment and wear *burqua* when going out.

## Adaptability of purdah

Purdah is flexible and varies according to practical and social contexts. In some instances men who are not blood relatives but adopted members of the family, such as neighbours, are allowed in to the harem. The point of the exercise is that once everyone is aware of the ground rules, adaptations are made to suit the situation. For instance in certain parts of the Subcontinent, across the religious divide, daughters-in-law observe purdah from their fathers- and brothers-in-law. In other circles it is enough for the daughter-in-law to cover her head. A woman observing purdah outside the home could be completely covered including hands, feet and face, or simply wear a transparent scarf over her head as a symbolic gesture, or do no more than avoid direct eye contact with a 'strange' man.

Purdah among the Asian Muslims in Britain is interesting. The bulk of the population came from rural backgrounds where purdah traditionally was restricted to a very small group of women, usually of high social standing. Women of the peasant or artisan class were often engaged in work with the men in the fields or elsewhere. Men and women in a Punjabi or Kashmiri village would be attired similarly, the only difference being, perhaps, *duputta* for women a and for men a turban wrapped round the head rather than draped over it. In effect the turban covered the head more fully than the duputta. Women would also be able to go about their business freely in the village, whether fetching water from the well or shopping. This pattern appears to be repeated in other areas of the Islamic world. Lina Fruzzetti (1981) reports that for rural women in Sudan, land owned by the government is allocated to villagers depending on their capacity to farm it and work is shared equally between men and women in the household. 'Though the majority of people in the country are of Islamic faith,' she observes, 'culturally the women in the rural areas enjoyed a freer status in the public domain than in the more urbanised areas'.

Rural women who come to urban situations adopt the habits perceived to be in keeping with the new environment. Asian women in urban Britain are soon seen to withdraw from men outside their family circle. What is even more fascinating is that whilst some women are happy running their shops in the middle of a busy market, when they attend functions within the Muslim community, they insist that men and women are segregated. This thinking is symbolised by draping a curtain to separate men from women at some weddings and public meetings. Sometimes the second generation women in the West go further, and insist on tying a thick scarf tightly over their heads; for them, their mothers' chiffon *duputta* is not Islamic enough. The adoption of purdah may signify an increase in their social status for women who came from the Subcontinent or elsewhere, but for those born in

Britain, it can be a reaction against a racist society which undermines their culture and religion. Purdah in the form of a scarf and harem in the form of a room in a house or a curtain in a public setting can signify women's space in which they are free. It may indeed be that they only wish to observe privacy from men who are their social peers and with whom future familial or social relations are possible, as Rebecca did in the Old Testament. It is reminiscent of a Western woman being happy to interact with the milkman or a plumber with her hair in curlers and wearing a housecoat, but rushing to dress more appropriately at the sight of someone she wants to impress, or someone whose opinion of her counts in her social standing. Interestingly, in the major cities of the Subcontinent weddings are held in *shadi* or marriage halls where families share tables just as at marriage receptions in Western communities.

Harem has certainly been used to challenge authority. Hudda Shaarawi's *Harem Years* describes how women across religious divides in Egypt used their own space of the harem to organise a successful campaign against colonialism after World War I. In the struggle both men and women were needed and were allowed to forget the tradition of the harem and join in.

> ...We women held our first demonstration (...) to protest the repressive act and intimidation practised by the British Authority. In compliance withthe roles of authority we announced our plans to demonstrate in advance but were refused permission... (Shaarawi, 1986).

A similar picture emerges in the Subcontinent during the struggle for independence. Women both used their private space to organise and abandoned it when necessary, for instance when women had to organise and address public meetings in the absence of their men, many of whom were imprisoned by the British. Perhaps the most noteworthy example is Bi Amma, the mother of Mohammed Ali, who addressed an all-male meeting of the Muslim League in 1917 when her son was imprisoned by the British. In 1921 at a similar public meeting of the organisation in Lahore, she lifted her veil because she found it cumbersome. Her decision to dispense with the veil met with little opposition. It may be because as an older woman speaking on behalf of her son, she was perceived as asexual and no threat to patriarchy, or that the goal of achieving national liberation was greater than that of observing traditional signs of gender demarcation. In any case, as a political leader, her challenge to wearing the veil met with little opposition.

The changes to purdah in Saudi Arabia at the time of *Hajj*, the pilgrimage to Mecca – one of the five pillars of Islam – or *Umrah*, a similar pilgrimage of lesser importance, are particularly noteworthy. At the time of *Hajj* or *Umrah* Muslim men and women together perform *tawaph* or circumambulation of the *Kabaah*. This tradition has been in existence for over two millennia, before the Old Testament and monotheism. From the advent of Islam there has been no segregation of the sexes in Mecca or Medina Mosques, the focal points of Islam. Furthermore, all pilgrims for *Hajj* or *Umrah* are duty bound to make their intention or *niah* for the pilgrimage at Masjid Ayesha, the mosque of Ayesha, the youngest wife of the prophet. This mosque, like others in Mecca and Medina and surrounding districts, for example Masjid Fatima, showed no signs of partitions until recently. But from 1992 the Masjid Nabwi, the Prophet's mosque in Medina, acquired a large new extension which segregated along gender lines, and the old mosque was partitioned for males and females. The Kabaah remains untouched by this new wave of exclusion, but attempts are being made in the mosque proper, which surrounds the Kabaah, to place bookcases along the various corridors and passage-ways to separate the sexes. The ultimate irony is the partitioning of Masjid Ayesha, the smaller part being allocated for women.

The reasons for this sudden shift are a matter for speculation. One possible explanation could be that as Saudi Arabia became more affluent through its oil revenue, it was more exposed to wider international cultural influences, especially those of the West, which may be perceived by the orthodox religious élite as decadent. Just as purdah was used to separate respectable women in imperial Iran from those representing lascivious pleasures, the Saudi élite has tried to guard against the inevitability of an opulent society by restricting its social pivot, the mosque.

The Arab world is currently convulsed by the debate between radical and liberal Muslims on how Islam should be practised in the twentieth century. Saudi Arabia, a traditional monarchy in which are situated the holiest shrines and cities of Islam, is dominated by the traditional strictures of the Wahabi sect. It is also the strongest ally of the West in the Middle East, assisting greatly, mostly in financial terms, in the recent war with Iraq which replaced on the throne the almost equally traditional Kuwaiti royal family. Radical Muslims attack the growing American cultural influences in the region and believe monarchies to be un-Islamic. But even within this gender-separated society, there are 3,000 women members of the Jeddah Chamber of Commerce. At a seminar held in the City of London in September 1995 to bring together Western companies and Arab businesswomen, a member of one of the Arab women delegations expressed surprise at 'the very small numbers of women on the Western delegations' (*Guardian*, October 1995).

Religious doctrine does not spring up in a vacuum. As it spreads to other cultures new customs are incorporated to give it local relevance. The acceptance of purdah in Iran and strict attitudes towards divorce/remarriage in medieval India are examples. Adaptation of religion to local custom is particularly clear in the Muslim adoption of a strict attitude to divorce in the Subcontinent. Divorce and remarriage are permitted in Islam, but were alien to medieval Hindu society. Whilst Muslims adopted the tradition of no divorce, wealthy Hindu women were increasingly in seclusion.

Nothing inherent in Islam dictates the banning of women from public life. In Abbasid Baghdad (750-1258 AD) women were poets and musicians, received foreign envoys, took part in state affairs and taught at Baghdad University. In Umayyad Spain women taught in Granada, Seville and Cordoba when the rest of Europe was in the 'Dark Ages'. In pre-communist China, Muslim women acted as instructors and led *juma* Friday prayers in female-only mosques, because it was considered demeaning for either sex to prostrate themselves before the other (Beck and Keddie, 1978).

Women of the ruling élite in the Ottoman Empire became heads of vast patronage networks that at times gave them direct control over the state apparatus. The daughter of Suleyman I and the widow of Grand Vizier Rustem are reputed to be responsible for the Ottoman's attempt to seize Malta in 1565 and themselves paid to fit out 400 warships for the purpose (Beck and Keddie, 1978).

Upper-class women in the Subcontinent in the nineteenth and early twentieth centuries who lived in the *zanana* travelled in their own curtained carriages. On trains they hired whole compartments which had curtains on the windows. Many abandoned both the zanana and purdah in the struggle against British colonial rule. Some, like Mohammed Ali Jinnah's sister, Fatmah Jinnah, Shaista Ikramullah, Begum Liaqat Ali Khan and Jawaher Lal Nehru's daughter, Indira Ghandi, entered national politics and other women eventually took their seats in parliament. Others joined professions which enabled them to work in female-only hierarchies, particularly in teaching and medicine. None of the women I interviewed in the Subcontinent or Britain observed strict purdah; having a female-only place of work was, however, an issue for both groups. Women in India and Pakistan who otherwise would not have worked outside the home were encouraged to do so by the availability of a 'safe environment'.

The institution of purdah then, is neither a pre-requisite of Islam nor confined to Islamic societies; it exists for a host of complex reasons. It differentiates upper-class women from working-class; it transcends religious boundaries; it is practised in a socio-economic and historical context. Purdah is subject to fashion and to economic and political circumstances. The struggle for independence brought upper-class women out of the purdah into the streets to follow political careers. (Shiasta Ikramullah recalls with nostalgia in her autobiography the years she was in purdah before entering into national politics in Pakistan (Ikramullah, 1963)). Once it became acceptable for 'respectable' women to earn money, what mattered was the type of work they did. Women working in female-only professions could be in purdah and still earn a living. The fashion changes constantly and with it the attitudes of women who practise it. None of these subtleties is recognised in the Western stereotypes of the Muslim woman.

Whilst purdah is generally associated with the Orient, and can be interpreted as keeping women hidden away or completely covered up, this is a superficial interpretation. A deeper analysis of its manifestation in the psycho-social relations between men and women is needed. Women in the West are considered freer than in the East, particularly in the world of Islam, and movement between the sexes is portrayed as totally unrestricted. Yet Western women are expected to conform to a dress code appropriate to their situation. For instance, Prime Minister Margaret Thatcher invariably wore a suit with a high-necked blouse so as to be taken seriously, just as Benazir Bhutto covered her head in public when Prime Minister of Pakistan. Lower down the social scale, scanty dress may be acceptable for a young woman in a night club, but not in a board meeting. Quintessentially purdah is the covering of women's bodies to make them asexual, just like the habits of nuns in the West. In other words, they enter men's world of work on the terms defined for them. This means the more covered-up a woman is, the more 'respectable', and this varies from one culture to another and from one context to another within the same culture. To be taken seriously and for their opinions to carry the same weight as men's, their bodies must be concealed. Research shows that in formal meetings women are more likely to be interrupted by men and less likely than men to have their ideas adopted. They may be physically sharing the same space but in reality an invisible barrier is all too evident. Essentially this is no different from women being allocated a physical place in which to operate in the Subcontinent or within the Asian communities in the West. Indeed, women in the West are beginning to see the value of having separate space.

## Sati

Early travellers, such as Alexander the Great, Marco Polo and the Islamic Middle Eastern Europeans, recorded the practice of sati in their travelogues, some with horror and others with fascination. There were attempts to curb it, by Emperor Akbar the Great in the sixteenth century, Shahjahan in the seventeenth and the British in 1829. The act and the notion of sati remain controversial in India and beyond. Accounts which have come down to us have mostly been written by travellers and outside observers; the reporting of the event is always highly charged. It is difficult to disentangle the different threads to work out what was the reality and what the myth.

The Sanskrit word *sati* appears to have derived from the verb root *sat* meaning 'real, true and virtuous' (Hawley, 1994). It has become an icon for loyalty, self-sacrifice and purity and a point of reverence for subsequent generations. It refers to the person, but in the vernacular *sati* can also be used for the action: the woman complying with the pure act of sati becomes sati in the process. There were two kinds of sati: dying with, *Sahamarana*, and dying away or separate, *Anumarana*.

The latter applied to widows considered to be 'impure' (menstruating or pregnant). Such a widow would die with a representation of her husband such as a turban or shoes rather then physically with him on the funeral pyre. *Anumarana* was much practised by the warrior classes, especially when the husband had died on the battlefield, but is a lesser form of sati.

Sati can be seen as a noble and courageous act – or as the ultimate manifestation of patriarchal control over women and their sexuality. It enables property and wealth to pass on to the man's relatives, including his children, rather than being inherited by his widow. One theory is that as societies became patriarchal and patrilineal, women lost their position of power and were viewed as chattels or property to be disposed of at the will of their masters. Polygyny was rooted in this belief, and demanded female sexual fidelity (Kelsey and Kelsey, 1991). Although associated with Islam, polygyny is not peculiar to it. When a woman enters into self-immolation at her husband's death the possibility of sexual infidelity to her deceased husband is instantly eliminated. Through the act of sati she can expiate her sins, become sati and follow her husband to an imagined heaven. Indeed, she has a 'baptism of fire' not just for herself but for her husband too, rather like Jesus Christ being crucified to absolve others of their sins. Thus a woman whose body and its functions have from ancient times been associated by men with shame, sin and temptation can become purified, ensuring spiritual bliss for herself and her husband. In sati, it is a clear mark of male dominance and vanity that a woman's life was not worth living without her man and master. As this awful rite was chiefly an appendage to princely state, it has been considered as honourable in itself and as reflecting additional lustre on the caste and family to which the victim belonged. Women have internalised the notion of devotion to the husband by giving their lives.

By the wife becoming sati not only would she relieve the family of the burden of supporting her, she would contribute to their wealth by enabling them to inherit the wealth of the deceased. Sins of both husband and wife are said to be expiated and the woman not only follows her husband to Valhalla – the imagined heaven – but acquires deification on earth; thus immortalised (Angiras, quoted in Altekar, 1973). Another theory suggested by Diodrus Siculus is that the rite was invented to prevent wives from poisoning their husbands.

The act of sati, like other human behaviours, is not simple or one-dimensional; it is affected by the individual's own attitude to the notion of purification by burning alive. She may find attractive the idea of being immortalised in this world by becoming elevated to the status of a goddess, whom people from the length and breadth of the country come to worship in a specially erected temple, an enduring reminder of her sacrifice and her relationship with her deceased husband, to whom she shows such loyalty. So she might step onto the pyre voluntarily – or she might be forcibly pushed by the relatives who stand to gain from her death, whether directly by inheriting property or from the kudos and prestige associated with this honourable act by a member of the family. Or there may be indirect material benefits: it has even been alleged that the family may have shares in the business which flows from establishing a pilgrimage centre in the memory of sati, such as accommodation, souvenirs and other commercial commodities.

## The history of sati

There is no consensus amongst scholars about the origin of sati. Some (e.g. Walker, 1968) postulate that it derived from the ancient Indo-Aryan custom of burying a few of his important possessions with the deceased. There was an ancient belief that the next life was a reflection of this one so the needs would be similar – as demonstrated by the Egyptian Pharaohs who had their most valued belongings buried with them together with animals, attendants and women who accompanied them in death and were buried in an adjoining burial chamber. The most extreme example of this practice has been recorded in Mesopotamia, where a series of royal tombs were filled with the bodies of those who had been chosen to accompany the king and queen in death. In one, RT217, lay the bodies of six men-servants, four women harpists and sixty-four ladies of the court (Woolley and Moorey, 1992).

Among the warrior classes in ancient times it was considered an affront to the memory of the deceased and an evident lack of devotion when a widow showed reluctance to accompany her husband's body to the pyre. The custom was well-established by the fourth century BC in Punjab, as recorded by Alexander the Great. But it was not universally applicable. In southern India it was introduced by brahminical civilisation and practised in their kingdoms, but it was prohibited in Malabar where matriarchy prevailed – of course sati applied only to women.

Sati was practised amongst the northern Indian Rajputs and warrior nations, where it reached drastic proportions in which wives, concubines, widows, sisters, mothers, sisters-in-law and their near relatives burnt themselves with the deceased. This rite developed into *jauhar,* which took place amongst various communities at the time of some great catastrophe to save the honour of females and the clan. The first instance of *jauhar* recorded in Greek chronicles took place after the capture by Alexander the Great of one of the towns of the Agalassoi tribe, when 20,000 citizens burnt themselves alive, with wives and children. Similarly, when Rajputs were certain to be defeated by the enemy, they would gather together their women and children and set them alight before meeting their death on the battlefield. A notable example occurred in 1303 when Khalizi Sultan, Ala-ud-din, attacked Chitar in his effort to possess Padamini, the beautiful Rajput princess of Marwar. As defeat became inevitable, Padamini and the other women of the fortress were burnt to death before the men advanced to the battlefield to meet their end (Walker,

41

1968). In a similar way, Cleopatra and two of her ladies-in-waiting chose to commit suicide as Egypt fell to the armies of Octavian, rather than face humiliation as captives (Flamarion, 1997).

The first recorded instance of sati in Indian epics is the reference to Madri, who ascended the funeral pyre of her husband Pandu even though sages tried to dissuade her from this unrighteous act. They did not succeed and four of his wives jumped in and were immolated (Walser, 1968). Sita too wanted to show her devotion to Rama, when Ravana's magic made her believe that he had been slain, by declaring her wish to burn with her husband.

The Puranas relate the story of Sati, Daksha's daughter and widow of Shiva. Sati enters the fire as a protest against the insults her husband received at the hands of her own father. By entering the fire herself, she shows her ultimate loyalty to her husband. In one version of the story, Sati is reborn as Parvati. In another, Shiva takes Sati's body from the fire and carries it around the world; each dismembered part, falling to the ground, forms a shrine. It is probable that this story has its origins in grassroots traditions of local goddesses. Certain areas, for example among Rajput cultures, have a strong tradition of Sati worship. It exists also in certain castes, for example the Aggarwal caste of successful merchants. Shrines and small sati stones are to be found in many parts of the Subcontinent, especially in the modern states of Maharashtra, Karnataka, Gujarat and Rajastan, where for centuries communities have been engaged in conflict in order to protect their trade routes or agricultural land from invading peoples. These temples depict icons of warriors killed on battlefields defending their people, with their wives lying beside them on the funeral pyre.

Lindsey Harlan, in her study of Rajput women in Rajastan, identifies three main sets of beliefs contributing to the cult of sati (Harlan in Hawley, 1994). They are the notions of *pativrati*, *sativrati* and *satimata*. *Pativrati*, from *pati* (husband) and *vrat* (vow), denotes a wifely devotion to the husband whom she must protect and encourage to reach his full potential. By fasting for her husband she enlists the support of deities in protecting her husband from all evils including death. The death of a *pativrati's* husband reflects on her lack of effort and this can be rectified by the act of sati. Self-immolation is proof of her *sat* or purity which transforms *sativrati* into *satimata* or pure mother. The idea of purifying a woman and elevating her to the status of a godhead by making her into a mother figure, sexually pure, is not confined to Hinduism. In Islam heaven is believed to lie at the mother's feet. In Christianity, Mary mother of Christ is sexually pure. She has borne a son outside of the act of sexual union necessary for mere mortals.

As in the case of purdah, women of lower social strata emulate sati in order to bring prestige to their families. This elevation of social status can then be passed on to subsequent generations.

Scholars are clear that sati was neither indigenous to India nor practised exclusively by followers of Hinduism.

> The custom of the sacrifice of the widow at the funeral of her husband was widely prevailing in ancient times. There is no direct evidence to show that it prevailed in the Indo-European age, but the fact that it was practised among the Gauls, the Goths, the Norwegians, the Celts, the Slavs and Thracians would justify the inference that it was probably well-established amongst the Indo-Europeans. It was quite common amongst the Scythians (Altekar, 1973).

Vincent Smith (quoted in Thompson, 1928) agrees that it was probably a Scythian rite introduced from central Asia.

It has been suggested that widow-burning was more widely practised – among, for instance, Tongans, Fijians, Maoris, and many African tribes. The Scandinavian legend of Balder refers to Nanna who ascended her husband's funeral pyre and Narse's version of the Volsunga saga makes Brunhilda sati. In the Greek legend of Thebes one of the seven wives of Capanenus was burnt with her husband.

In Vedic times it appears that there was a symbolic ceremony: the widow of the chief lay with the body of her husband but was allowed to rise and marry her husband's brother and continue to produce children. This custom, known as *levirate*, is referred to in the Bible, as a way to ensure that children were brought up in the name of a deceased husband.

Like the institution of purdah or harem, sati is not integral to one Eastern faith nor confined to Hindus. It developed or declined according to the needs of the time. The *Padmapurana* extolled the custom but prohibited it for Brahmins. If anyone was caught helping in the act they were deemed guilty of murder. From the twelfth to fourteenth century AD Brahmins followed the act. It seems to have increased between 1680 and 1830. Scores of women burnt themselves on men's funeral pyres. It was adopted by other groups, amongst them Muslims and Sikhs, and though condemned by the third Guru, it increased in the last decades of his life (Walker, 1968). It also increased during British expansion in Bengal despite efforts by Rammohun Roy (1772-1833) to prohibit it. If women died with their husbands, the family's land could eventually be incorporated into the British state. This was done with the support of Hindu priests who were ready to impress upon the women their duty to their religion and their deceased husbands, as we saw in chapter 1.

When the body of Ranjit Singh was cremated in 1839 during the Moghul Raj, four of his wives and seven concubines were burnt with him. Sati, like purdah, was not uniformly followed by all women expected to bear *sat*. Voices of dissent from women and men were raised long before the British Raj. Women who refused to follow their husband's funeral pyre were tied to planks of wood or dragged there to ensure submission. But sati was condemned in some Sanskrit texts on the science of righteousness (*dharmashastra*) and by the Moguls as well as other enlightened forces, male and female, within Indian society, historically and today.

The Sanskrit poet Bana wrote in AD 650:

> The custom is a foolish mistake of stupendous magnitude, committed under the reckless impulse of despair and infatuation. It does not help the dead for he goes to heaven or hell according to his deserts. It does not ensure reunion since the wife who has uselessly sacrificed her life goes to the hell reserved for suicide. By living she can still do much good both to herself by pious work and to the departed by offering libations for his happiness in the other world. By dying she only adds to her misery (quoted in Walker, 1968).

Or in the words of Akbar, quoted by Abdul Fazil in *Happy Sayings of His Majesty*: 'It is a strange commentary on the magnanimity of men that they should seek their deliverance though the self-sacrifice of their wives' (Thompson, 1928). Hinmun and Raja Rammohun Roy, social reformers in the nineteenth century, also opposed the custom; and yet the general perception in the West is that it is a religious rite of universal application to all Hindus and was accepted without question until the British outlawed it in 1833. As there was no theological sanction for sati, Hindu priests who wanted to give the rite a religious justification changed the wording in the scriptures to suit their purpose. The original Rig Veda says:

> 'Arohantu janaya yomin agre' (Let the mothers advance to the altar first)

By changing the 'agre' (before) to 'agneh' (fire), sati appears to be sanctioned:

> 'Arohantu janayo yomin agneh' (Let the mothers go into the void of the fire)

Max Muller, quoted in Thompson (1928), calls this change to the text 'perhaps the most flagrant instance of what can be done by an unscrupulous priesthood'. Raja Rammohun Roy used this evidence of scriptural tampering by priests to support his campaign against sati in Bengal during the British Raj.

In Bengal, unlike in most of the rest of the North India, widows were entitled to their husbands' share of family land and wealth. It may be for this reason that the British authorities tacitly allowed the practice to continue unabated – that is until it became a political issue. The custom reinforced the tendency of the British to regard all Indians as savage and barbaric, with bizarre customs especially towards their women. The practice was not equated, then or now, with sending young men to their deaths through the glorification of war. The practice of sati was partly for socio-economic reasons; the victims were either without choice or they internalised their sacrifice as essential and one which would glorify them.

The vows of celibacy for Christian and Buddhist monks and nuns, the beating of the chest by Shi'ite Muslims to commemorate the death of Imam Hussain (grandson of the Prophet Muhammad) and, in any society, going to war, are all examples of such purification of the soul by sacrificing physical needs and desires, a thread which runs through most human societies. It appears that human beings have a dichotomous love/hate relationship with themselves; the mind/soul versus body. It may be rooted in the search for or belief in permanence, eternal existence beyond the lifespan of the body, which is only attained through sacrificing pleasures; and the ultimate denial is offering one's body for a higher cause: one's country, love, a deity or a friend. Such ideals could be achieved by the individual making a voluntary sacrifice induced by socialisation and propaganda or forced by circumstances. In other words, an honourable death may be preferable to a life of misery, poverty and the taunts of peers, relatives or neighbours.

## The colonial legacy

During the colonial period Hindu reformists and Christian missionaries joined forces to bring about changes in the practice of sati; Christian missionaries in particular had portrayed the widow as a powerless and abject victim. The East India Company wanted to rescue her so that she might be saved from her own people. This portrayal also served to reinforce the notion of the superiority of the colonial civilisation. This view is supported by Rajan and Figueira: 'Whilst outraging Western sensibilities and exploiting Western curiosity about the grotesque and barbarian, the sati's existence satisfied European nostalgia for the East or lost innocence'. (Dorothy Figueira in Hawley, 1994)

Rajan (1993) postulated that by prohibiting sati in India in 1833, William Patrick was reinforcing the notion of the superiority of British civilisation which condescended to save the Hindu woman victim. Although the women's movement in England was gaining ground, chastity and fidelity were important components of sati, on which English women's behaviour could be modelled. Though sati was perceived to be 'Hindu' in origin, it could be fed into different ideologies.

Present-day occurrences of sati are sensationalised in the Western media, thus creating the classic 'otherness' and reinforcing the notion of Western (i.e. white European) racial and religious superiority. Rajan offers the experience of Roop Kanwar, an 18 year old widow, as a case study of how the forces of patriarchy and neo-colonialism continue to maintain the otherness of 'ethnic minority' women in the West. On 4 December 1987, Roop Kanwar, who had been married only seven months, died on her husband's funeral pyre in Deorala village near Jaipuri Rajastan. The event made headline news on the front page of the *New York Times*, as had the news a few years earlier of a woman stoned to death in a Middle Eastern country for adultery. 'The monolithic 'Third World Women' as a subject instantaneously becomes an over-determined symbol, victim not only of universal patriarchy but also of specific third world religious fundamentalism' (Rajan, *op.cit.*).

Roop Kanwar's case, or rather national and international reaction to it, highlights the manifold schools of thought which the institution of sati represents. It appears to be no less controversial in the twentieth century than it has been for over a millennium. It continues to invite social comment and generate heated debate between the traditionalist lobby, some of whom believe it to be a religious rite worthy of deification, and the liberal school, which views it as the epitome of male vanity in destroying female life. Roop Kanwar's own attitude to the event, as so often in such cases, remains unrecorded. But even if it were, its authenticity would be questionable amidst the media interest such a case provoked. That over three hundred thousand people were reported to have attended the *chunari mahotsav* (a function marking the thirteenth day after sati) is testimony to the interest generated. Although illegal, as it has been for over a century, sati continues. The government proved helpless to act effectively and press charges against those arrested for taking part. The wealthy businessmen in Hindu society who argued that the banning of sati constituted an infringement of their religious rights were able to erect a temple in Deorala village, which has become a pilgrimage centre, thus clinching what Rajan (*ibid.*) calls 'religious sanction, political complicity and economic benefit, (which) have combined to encourage a cult of sati in a climate of overall oppression of women'.

The institution of sati epitomises men's control over women's wealth, minds, bodies and their lives. All this is given a coating of respectability by rendering sati synonymous with 'pious' and 'piety'. The material representation of the ideal 'pure' woman loyal to the memory of her deceased husband, in the form of temples and the promise of reaching eternal bliss, contributes to its continuation. A glorified death with promise of salvation is made preferable to a life of misery and responsibility. Other women are also said to benefit by coming to the temple of sati seeking answers to their problems.

The sacrifice of one's life for a higher cause is not unique to Hinduism. It runs through most human societies, expressed as religious martyrdom or dying for one's country. As Napoleon Bonaparte is reported to have said, 'I have made a remarkable discovery. Men will die for ribbons.' In other words, people who would not take risks for material gain might be prepared to give their lives for social recognition. The basic human need to be immortalised and achieve posterity is an important ingredient in the cult of sati. The mortal body can be sacrificed for a cause which is eternal, thus immortalising the giver. Christ, for dying on the cross to expiate the sins of humankind and remembered for it, is a case in point. Recent mass suicides by cult members anticipating transmutation to a higher plane as the millennium approaches spring from the same impulse. Finally, the need for and attitude to sati, as war, is often dictated by the needs of society to which individuals react differently. Some are compelled to take part by force of circumstance; others may enter into it willingly for economic or psychological gains.

Purdah and sati are both, in different ways, manifestations of a single male impulse: the need to control women's space, their bodies – especially their sexuality – and their minds. Somehow men never resolve their relationship with their mothers. All their subsequent relationships with women are a reflection of the dichotomy of the love and hatred for that figure. They react to them either by making them sexually so 'pure' that they are elevated to the status of a goddess or so 'impure' that they deserve their contempt. Purdah and sati can, in the final analysis, be seen as tests to determine into which of these categories a woman falls.

## Arranged marriages

The concept of arranged marriages as applied to Asians carries connotations of coercion and lovelessness. Taken out of context and sensationalised, the custom is contrasted with Western marriages, which, in this argument, are contracted solely for love. It is assumed that Christianity, seen as synonymous with Western civilization, is a religion which allows individual freedom; whereas Eastern religions, particularly Islam, deny individual freedom even in this very private area of life. Yet the system of arranged marriages is neither exclusive to nor uniformly practised by all Asians, in the Subcontinent or elsewhere. Marriage, like other social institutions, is subject to fashion, social trends and the socio-economic position of the couple. The higher the status of the families concerned, the greater the chances of stringent rules being applied. This appears to be a general pattern across the world. Marriage is a social contract which has wider implications than romantic love.

The tradition of arranged marriage is an ancient one, known to have existed in many societies, such as the noble classes in Pharaomic Egypt. It was designed to keep intact the wealth and social standing of the family. The higher the status of the individuals concerned, the greater the care taken to ensure the suitability of marriage partners. It was not unknown for the monarch to marry his or her own sibling, or an offspring (Watterson, 1991). Rameses II and Tutankhamun both married their half-sisters. A part from ensuring the political lineage which could be passed through either male or female lines, this prevented the divine bloodline from being sullied by lesser beings. These marriages were not necessarily conjugal, but always received precedence over subsequent marriages or relationships which might produce children. For instance, the eighteen-year old Cleopatra married her ten year old brother Ptolemy 13, according to Ptolemaic dynastic law. Although this marriage was only contractual, her subsequent marriage to another brother and her relationships with Mark Antony and Julius Caesar were subordinated to it (Flamarion, 1997).

The separation of the concept of marriage from that of romantic love prevailed in medieval Europe; marriages were largely a matter of business. The notion of courtly love – romantic platonic love for an unattainable woman – was exalted in song and story. For royal and aristocratic marriages, political expediency and economic advantage were the rule. The poor had their own concerns, usually the need to ensure that the prospective wife was fertile.

The British applied practicality to their rule in India. From the beginning, the charms of Asian women resulted in partnerships with British men, not all sanctified by formal marriage. Some civil marriages contracted between an Indian woman and a British man were not recognised. Almost inevitably these unrecognised marriages were abandoned, to be superseded by an officially approved marriage with a British woman.

The British mass media, the general population and even educationalists often assume that an 'arranged marriage' means a coerced marriage, or a marriage of convenience, thus reinforcing the notion of Asian woman as victim. The 'arranged marriage' is regarded as loveless and peculiar to the Asian community, and the implication is that white British women have complete freedom in their choice of partner. The reality, as Ikramullah (1963) observed, is somewhat different:

> What is new is the idea of love-match rather than arranged marriage. Amongst the older nations marriages were looked upon as social institutions and as such were not to be entrusted to the fleeting fancy of youth but to the mature judgement of elders.

As marriage is a social arrangement with prospects of children and inheritance, considerable care is taken to ensure the suitability of the partner. In some cases, marriages in the West are arranged in much the same way as Asian marriages, the degree of arrangement usually shaped by the perceived social and/or economic importance of the marriage partners. British royalty tries to maintain its exclusivity thus; other groups, such as the most observant Jewish communities, apply stringent rules of arranged marriage to preserve their unique identity. Where the social institutions (families, lineage and clan) are strong, marriages are easier to arrange; where they are weak, the arrangement occurs through neighbourhood, class or education. Similarly but in more subtle ways, Western parents try to ensure that their children do not marry partners lower in social status. In an English middle-class family a conversation could go something like this:

> Father to daughter: 'John's a nice boy, but not really your type, darling. What happened to Dr George's son who went up to Cambridge to read Law? Much more your kind of person'.

The effect of this somewhat indirect approach is much like Asian parents approaching members of their community and asking them to keep an eye out for a suitable match for their medical student daughter.

Even where arrangements are not overt, research findings show that most people in the West choose their partners from roughly the same socio-economic group. Most Asian parents take great care to match up the prospective marriage partners, but this fact is ignored in the Western interpretation. The degree to which the marriage is 'arranged' depends on the young people, the background of the family, their own attitudes and those of the local community, and applies both in the Subcontinent and Britain. A recent study on marriage carried out in Lahore found that 'the making of a proper match is an issue of ideology; the complementary nature of the man/woman married unit. This is expressed in terms of social and economic criteria' (Fischer in Hastings and Webner, 1991). Fischer observes that parents would go to great lengths to make an optimum match. For example, if they want their daughter to marry a doctor they would encourage her to pursue a medical career. This degree of care is taken not only because a bad marriage makes the couple unhappy but because it reflects on the family's *izzat* (honour). Fischers's sample of thirty three marriages yielded one love-match between people who were unrelated, although love-matches between cousins were not uncommon. The two systems produce roughly the same outcomes: some work, others do not. Some are fulfilling and others remain a social or economic convenience. This pattern is evident even when divorce is less of a stigma and is easier for women to obtain.

It is customary for Asian parents and other adults to play a major role in finding a partner for their child. This is done in a variety of ways, depending on the situation, from approaching close relatives, friends or neighbours to approaching complete strangers. The degree of arrangement also varies, from marrying close relatives, like first cousins in the case of Muslims and maternal uncles in the case of Hindus from Karnataka, to complete strangers for northern Indian Hindus. According to Shariah law, Muslim marriage cannot take place without free agreement between the partners. This assent has to be given in front of witnesses. Marriage without the consent of both partners is null and void. The precedent is the girl who came to the Prophet Muhammad complaining that she had been married without being consulted; he directed that she was free to have the marriage dissolved if she wished (Lemu and Heeren, 1987). Both men and women are able to propose marriage; the first marriage of the Prophet Muhammad was in response to a proposal by the older widow, Katija.

The misconception that an arranged marriage is at best forced, and at worst a marriage of convenience pervades the rules which govern the British immigration system. Marriages arranged between an Asian British partner and a spouse from the Subcontinent were subject until the change of government in 1997 to the 'primary purpose' rule, to ensure that the marriage was not for reasons of achieving entry into Britain. This 'primary purpose' clause, founded on the assumption that an arranged marriage is probably a loveless marriage of convenience, obliged the couple to prove beyond a reasonable doubt that the purpose of marriage was not economic advancement for the prospective husband (see Sachdeva, 1993). Naturally, the application of these rules severely curtailed Asian women's rights in marital arrangements.

The report of the Commission for Racial Equality of their formal investigation into immigration control procedures (1985) states that:

> the rules 'Instructions to Immigrations Officers' were amended to provide not just that admission could be refused on certain grounds, but that Commonwealth citizens could be admitted to join wives in the UK only if there were special considerations which made their exclusion undesirable.

The instructions stated that Commonwealth husbands could be admitted only if the Secretary of State was satisfied that there were 'special considerations, whether of a family nature or otherwise, which render exclusion undesirable'. On 'primary purpose' it comments: 'the current rules still discriminate between men and women insofar as settled status in the UK entitles a man to be joined by his wife or fiancee whereas a woman is so entitled only if she is a British citizen.' The 'primary purpose' rule was abolished in July 1997, but this has made no significant difference to the outcome because regulations governing the economic status of the sponsoring spouse remain unchanged. In other words as Asian women in Britain are disproportionately affected by unemployment they are not in a position to demonstrate their ability to support their husbands without recourse to the public purse.

Young Asian women in Britain must satisfy many complicated rules in order to qualify to bring a husband to Britain: they must have their own bank account, have a settled job and their own accommodation. Given these restrictive rules and regulations, many Asian women have to face the painful choice between higher education and securing paid employment. They often choose the latter, especially since it often takes several years for the spouse to be permitted to enter Britain to join them. There is an additional pressure to make such a marriage successful: if the marriage breaks down within two years, the spouse is deported, without right of appeal.

The system of arranged marriage now operates as an option which attracts many young Asian men and women; even when a prospective marriage partner has been identified, a formal process of 'arranging' the marriage may be followed. Importantly, for a large minority of Asian young people growing up in Britain, having their marriages arranged by their families is more than a social convenience. It can enable the parents or elders of the family or community to discharge their duty to their children to provide them with emotional security in the form of marriage. The rest of the family, which the marriage partners automatically draw on, can help to sustain a marriage. The arranged marriage system does not, of course, preclude marriage solely for romantic love outside of all the social norms. Nor does it assume a loveless marriage. Love is considered an important ingredient in the relationship – but is understood to develop and mature as the couple live with each other. Love is not taken for granted; it is expected to fluctuate like other human emotions, such as jealousy, greed, envy and hatred. In human relations everything is possible.

## Divorce

After the Second World War, the world order changed and, with it, the economic relationships between countries, within countries, and even in the family unit. Power shifted from the old empires of Britain and France to the new superpowers of America and the Soviet Union. Family life had been subject to great strain during the war, with long separations, and some marriages did not survive. Hasty wartime marriages led to an alarming rise in the divorce rate, and there was simultaneously a baby boom when men returned home. Since then the classical Western nuclear family, consisting of a married couple with children, has been in decline. In the US between 1960 and 1980, the percentage of such families fell from 44 per cent to 29 per cent. In other industrialised countries there was a similar decline of the nuclear family and the proportion of children born in wedlock, precipitating a great deal of noise from politicians and religious leaders, to no great effect. Fundamental social change has been attributed in the West to the women's liberation movement, the contraceptive pill and an increase in women's earning power.

> The astonishing 'great leap forward' of the (capitalist) world economy and its growing globalisation not only divided and disrupted the concept of a Third World, it also brought virtually all its inhabitants consciously into the modern world. (Hobsbawm, 1995).

In their preoccupation with the Western world, feminists fail to take account of the changes affecting the lives of Asian women in the Subcontinent and Britain. Those living in Britain who marry men from the Subcontinent may find their marital role totally changed. The men often cannot find work, and the women must show evidence of financial independence in order to convince the immigration authorities to allow their husbands to join them. In the Subcontinent a woman will live among a network of older women, usually relatives, to whom she can turn for help and support during times of difficulty. Such networks have proved difficult to recreate in the West, and this has led to noticeably higher rates of divorce and marital breakdown as women juggle onerous domestic and employment duties. The work of Rani Atma in founding the Asian Family Counselling service was a move to respond to this situation, but the resources of the Service are slender compared with the need.

The Asian family has been subject to as many changes as the Western family, and frequently under conditions of greater strain; yet a view prevails that nothing has changed. Divorce is more common, both in the Subcontinent and in the West. More diverse patterns of family existence are in evidence; women may choose not to marry, or to marry and have children while actively pursuing a career. Widows may head households, or each member of a family may elect to live in a separate family home. Since some of these changes are new within the Asian family, as with the Western family, it is the older generation that is finding it hardest to adjust.

Traditional Hindu women did not divorce, although marital breakdown is not unknown in Hindu society. In recent years the profound societal taboo against divorce has relaxed a little, as in most societies, although Hindu religious custom assumes that marriage is for life. Remarriage, for a divorced or widowed Hindu woman, is becoming more common in Britain. In the Indian Subcontinent disapproval of divorce by the majority Hindu community had its effect on Moghul and subsequent Muslim society; much stricter rules were applied to divorce, and it was increasingly frowned upon. Muslim women can institute a divorce suit for a variety of reasons; during the research discussed in the next chapter, several divorced women were interviewed.

The procedure of divorce in Islam is one in which great emphasis is placed on reconciliation. There are three stages. Traditionally, in a case of mutual consent or where the husband is seeking a divorce, a woman should wait three monthly cycles after the first pronouncement of divorce during which time her husband remains responsible for her welfare and maintenance. This is to ensure that she is not expecting a child; during this time she may, if she wishes, remain in the marital home. The family will make great efforts to reconcile the partners during this period, and if a reconciliation does occur, the divorce is automatically revoked. The same procedure follows for the second and the third pronouncement of divorce; after the third the divorce becomes irrevocable. The wife is free to remarry after the final three-month waiting period. The first husband is not permitted to remarry her unless she has in the meantime married another man and been divorced. If a woman is seeking a divorce against the wishes of her husband she may take her case to court and obtain divorce.

Like Orthodox Jewish women, Muslim women will seek religious divorce in addition to a civil divorce. The dowry gift from her husband remains hers, even in the case of divorce, and he still has the responsibility of maintaining the children of the marriage. Any money that she earns remains hers exclusively, as does any dowry gift from her parents on marriage. A Muslim widow or divorcee may marry whomever she wishes, being regarded as sufficiently mature and experienced to decide for herself.

Attitudes to divorce often reflect a community's attitude towards marriage. For Christians marriage is made by divine law, only to be terminated at death.

> But from the beginning of the creation God made them male and female. For this cause shall a man leave his father and mother, and cleave to his wife; And they twain shall be one flesh: so then they are no more twain but one flesh. What therefore God hath joined together, let no man put asunder. (Mark 10: 6-9)

For Hindus, marriage is a sacrament not severed at death but taken to eternity. For Muslims it is a social contract, the details of which can be mutually agreed and written in. However, as communities live together over time, their habits and life style mingle and affect each other's attitudes and behaviour. Nowhere is it more true than in attitudes to marriage and divorce. Muslim attitudes towards divorce in the Subcontinent became stricter to match those of the majority Hindus. Since the Second World War, break-up of marriages has become more widespread and accepted across the world. Immigration procedures – which can take years – can exacerbate pressure on the marriage and precipitate divorce. This additional factor has contributed to the adoption of a more relaxed attitude towards marriage break-up in the Asian community.

Dowry, initially a benign gift to the bride by her Hindu parents, is now common among Sikhs and Muslims also. In the last century, the practice has become a problem both on the Subcontinent and in the West. The problem in the West is that dowry gifts can become excessive (see Menski, 1998) but death as a result of dowry disputes is not unknown. In certain areas of the Subcontinent however, notably Punjab, Utar Pradesh and Delhi, dowry-related murders and 'assisted' suicides occur in their thousands each year notwithstanding legislation in 1961 forbidding dowry giving. Brides are put to death, generally by burning, by the groom's family, because the girl's parents have failed to satisfy the demands for dowry by the husband and his family (Menski, 1998).

The regulation of women, by both the prevailing religious ideology and the state, is often oppressive, despite the overt aims of the religion and of the state. An Ortho-dox Jewish woman, even if divorced in British law, may not be free to remarry if her ex-husband stands on his right to refuse her a religious divorce and Muslim women can find themselves in a similar position.

This chapter demonstrates that sati, purdah and arranged marriages are not integral to Hinduism, Islam or Sikhism, but are social customs which predate the religions and which were simply incorporated into religious doctrine along with other tradi-tions of the day. Moreover, they are clearly not static; on the contrary, they are sub-ject to social change and national and international pressures.

# Chapter 4
# Asian Women in the Subcontinent

We lift the veil to let you see
The wonder world that we may be.
Struggle though our life be
Don't forget similarity between us and thee.

The 'Asian women' stereotype camouflages the underlying similarities in the position of women across ethnic, social and cultural boundaries, as my study of the position of Asian women in the Subcontinent reveals. Women encounter a host of common problems irrespective of socio-economic system and ideology even though, as MacDonald (1976) remarks, 'each country has distinctive social expectations and legal norms defining appropriate female activities and cultural values which affect women's aspirations for meaningful status inside and outside the home'. The status of women cannot be assumed on the basis of industrialisation, nor can it be assumed that universal suffrage has allowed women greater participation in the public sphere and politics. Capitalist, socialist and 'mixed' economies all reveal severe cases of gender discrimination, especially when one looks beyond the few newly privileged women in prominent positions.

To investigate these issues in greater detail, I examined the position of women in teaching, retailing, finance and garment manufacturing in the Indian Subcontinent. I focused on urban rather than rural women because the research suggests that 'Asian' women in the West have similar roles to urban women in the Subcontinent (Parmar, 1982; Allen and Wolkowitz, 1987; Commission for Racial Equality, 1988). In Britain, for instance, many had lived in an urban setting, often for three generations.

The bulk of the interviews were carried out in Karachi in Pakistan, with a few in the Indian cities of Bombay, Bangalore and Mysore, to compare and contrast the findings (see map, p.57). The field work concentrated on Pakistani Muslim women for a number of reasons. Pakistani Muslim girls in Britain appear consistently to underachieve educationally and in terms of careers. This is often viewed by educationalists and others as somehow integral to their culture and religious roles and expectations. It is generally assumed that their culture, in particular their religion, accords inferior status to women. The limited amount of freedom afforded them is seen as enshrined in the institution of purdah which is regarded as an inherent part of their religious doctrine. These assumptions are, as has been shown, erroneous.

I also examined the work patterns of a sample of women in the Subcontinent, to see whether these bore any resemblance to the stereotypes prevalent in the West. Empirical data was collected through interviewing women about their work and educational aspirations, and the data interpreted in the light of the stereotypes. Stereotypes of 'Asian' women dwell on the lack of control that they are supposed to have over their lives; by looking at work aspirations in relation to actual work situations, I tried to establish how much control they had in reality.

When examining the reality of parental aspirations and how these affect the daughter's own expectations, we must also examine the support given to the girls, including the role played by teachers and other adults. I looked at three sectors: the retail services including banking and insurance; the teaching profession; and manufacturing in the form of a clothing factory. These sectors were explored against the context of the general societal expectations of women, contrasting their situation with those of their Asian counterparts in the West, where racism is another issue to be contended with.

Control of one's own finance is viewed as a factor in women's liberation and independence, often translated by women in the West into women's right to work, although these are not necessarily synonymous. For one thing, women may not earn enough money to feel in control of their finances, and even when they are, it may go to someone else.

Conversely, non-earning women sometimes have control of the family's budget. The eldest woman in the household may be given all the earnings of the household, which gives her day-to-day financial control, but not financial independence. This may be important when a woman is divorced or widowed or for a young woman who does not want to get married. There appears to be little literature on women's control of finance; most studies have concentrated on the relationship between earning capacity and power within the household rather than the control of household finances and power (Pahl, 1989).

## Interviewing methods

Direct interviewing was decided upon for three reasons: firstly, because there is evidence to support the view that interviews have a greater success rate than postal

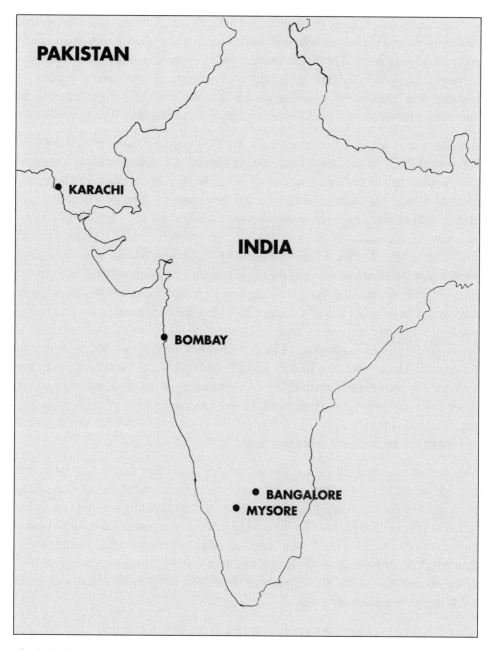

*The bulk of the interviews were carried out in Karachi in Pakistan, with a few in the Indian cities of Bombay, Bangalore and Mysore, to compare and contrast the findings.*

questionnaires in eliciting responses. Secondly, I found in practice that people tended to be more co-operative and forthcoming about their experiences when approached personally. Thirdly, it enabled me to assess the situation of the inter-viewees and pose questions accordingly, in as natural and free a manner as possible. For this reason I chose to use a semi-structured approach, asking questions without using a questionnaire (Ackroyd and Hughes, 1981).

All groups were asked the same questions but their wording and order depended on the context. For instance, when interviewing women in a clothing factory it seemed more appropriate to ask first how long they had worked in the place and how they came to choose that mode of livelihood and then about the kind of school they had attended. Such an action observer role, more commonly used by social anthro-pologists (Ackroyd and Hughes, 1981), seemed appropriate also because I stayed with some of the women I interviewed and became involved in their lives. One Parsi woman in Bombay arranged for me to sample a number of experiences in her life, including attending a Parsi wedding and wearing a *gara* which was a family heirloom. The *gara* is a sari of silk crêpe de Chine, hand-embroidered with a heavy border in an intricate design that is Chinese in influence. I was told that it symbolised the Parsi exodus from China, where they were persecuted at the turn of the century. Throughout their history in the Subcontinent, the Parsi community has attempted to preserve that memory by the embroidery of the *gara*, which is passed down from one generation to the next. I visited members of her family, including her sister, who married a Muslim and raised her children as Muslims whilst herself continued to practise the Zoroastrian faith.

This pattern of arranging for me to visit or stay with other family or friends and involve me in their daily lives was general in both India and Pakistan. One of my hosts in Bangalore facilitated my stay with her aunt in Mysore, who took me to her island of coconut palms. Another host in Hyderabad arranged for his son to accom-pany me to the bazaar when I went shopping and offered his friends' hospitality in Bombay. Interviews became not simply research tools but social events over a meal or snacks and cups of tea. Some, however, especially those conducted in shops and work-places, were less informal.

It was important to establish rapport with the interviewees and to feel 'accepted' and 'trusted'. There is always a conflict between creating rapport and maintaining a standardised objective interview style. The interviews were not intended to be a one-way process of eliciting information and maintaining detachment; rather they fol-lowed the approach described by Ann Oakley (1981): 'It becomes clear that in most cases the goal of finding out about people is best achieved when the relationship between interviewer and interviewee is non-hierarchical.' Interviews conducted in the comfort of someone's home could take the whole afternoon and others half an hour when women were called away from their customers in busy shops.

Organising interviews was not without problems, as the women's work schedules were heavy and transportation was often difficult for me. Field research can be logistically problematic. Some of the women interviewed were interested to know the purpose of the interview and in particular what effect the research would have on the lives of people in Britain and the benefits to their lives in the Subcontinent. The question of confidentiality also arose. These were matters which no researcher can afford to ignore. Research into social situations should lead to improvement rather than simply recording the status quo. In a very modest way, I hoped that whilst preserving the anonymity of the women interviewed, my research would add some insight into the lives of women in the Subcontinent and work towards breaking down some of the stereotypes held in the West.

The areas of education, retailing, finance and garment manufacturing were chosen because these areas most closely resembled those in which Asian women work in Britain (Allen and Wolkowitz, 1987). I made initial contact with women in these categories through my own social contacts, and they in turn gave me the names of other contacts. It was easier to establish an informal network of workers and ensure an informal working atmosphere than would have been possible with a random sample. This stratified snowball sample showed one way that the process of networking actually manifested itself.

The limitations of the interview sample, 52 women in all, are recognised and indicate tentative rather than conclusive findings. Although limited in scale due to sparse resources and considerable field work problems, the survey helps to establish parameters for future study, and might well yield useful insights.

In addition, having spent my childhood in Karachi I wanted to make use of my linguistic and cultural skills to broaden the understanding of the lives of women there. There was also the incentive of staying with members of my family, who had several contacts for interviews. Contacts in India were similarly made through friends and relatives. Bombay was chosen because of its closeness to Karachi and its historical development. To obtain a comparative southern perspective, I interviewed a small number of women in Bangalore and Mysore. All the interviews were conducted during the period 11 December 1987 to 26 January 1988, embracing local elections in Karachi and the reorganising of the city's educational system, and a five-day national mourning for the death of King Khan, a noted freedom fighter against the British, which coincided with celebrations of the 40th anniversary of Independence.

The interviews focused on the relationship between the women's aspirations and the outcomes – the relationship between dream and reality. Two aspects were concentrated upon: educational achievement and paid work, in the context of what was expected of the women in their familial roles and other social expectations. Women's identities and roles are often defined in terms of their relationship with male relatives and their prescribed social roles. Men are neither described nor con-strained by the same operational rules. In the words of Afshar (1985):

> The subordination of women is not only clearly seen in the context of the family. Ideologically, women are defined largely in terms of their familial relationship, whereas men frequently are not. Women as mothers, daughters, sisters are con-strained by an ideology that works as a form of control. Whilst men too have these constraints they are more likely to benefit from them when young and to be free from them when older.

Women's own perceptions of what they can reasonably expect are affected by these factors. Furthermore, women's life chances and their paid occupations in particular are influenced, often determined, by their families' occupational positions. Even when women's aspirations are confined to the field of paid work they seem to be problematic, for they have to be judged within the socio-political context in which they take place (Shaheed and Mumtaz, 1987). The women interviewed are located in an economy with a well-established agrarian sector as well as modern indus-trialised development. All interviews took place in urban settings.

The questions raised are as follows:

Why do women undertake paid work?

What do women feel about the role of paid work for themselves and other women?

What do men in a patriarchal society expect of women in respect of paid employ-ment?

What factors affect the fulfilling or thwarting of women's aspirations?

## Retailing – Meena Bazaar

Meena Bazaar is a women-only shopping complex established in Karachi about thirty years ago; all the shopkeepers/attendants and shoppers are women. It can be seen as a 'safe' environment which women control physically and economically, and in which they can excel in their various skills, or it could be seen as a 'safety valve' in a patriarchal and capitalist society, allowing women limited access to paid work whilst men retain the mainstream and high-powered positions.

Women themselves often saw the value of a women-only workplace. It serves three purposes: one is to win the support of families to allow their women to work there. Secondly, they in turn acted as role models, encouraging other women to take up employment. Thirdly, a women-only workplace is a supportive environment for women to work in.

Fifteen women who worked in the bazaar were interviewed. Women in this cate-gory came from a variety of backgrounds, ranging from very wealthy to quite poor.

This range was reflected in their educational backgrounds, their aspirations and their reasons for employment.

There does appear to be a tradition of women-only activities in the Subcontinent, the most famous being that of the Red Fort in Delhi in the Moghul era – the 16th century. Each Thursday evening women of the royal household would set out stalls of merchandise and dress up and act the parts of shopkeepers, purchasers and beggars, rather like Marie-Antoinette playing at milkmaids in the Petit Trianon. Unlike their later French counterparts, however, the Moghul women used poetry for all their interactions at these events, thus contributing to another Moghul tradition of *Mushaira* (a gathering of poets). The custom of separate activities for women was continued after Partition in 1947. In Pakistan there were separate days for women to visit exhibitions, zoos, museums or other public places. In India too the tradition continues in many areas, including co-operatives, education and banking, so there is quite a significant tradition of women-only facilities.

A mother and daughter were included among the interviewees. The older woman complained of her lack of chances to gain education when she was young; all preference had been given to her brother. Her mother had died when she was quite young; her father, who was a teacher, used to give tuition to other people's children but never taught her. He had lavished attention and praise on her brother but expected her to look after the household after her mother's death. She was also expected to continue to look after her father and his needs, even after her own marriage. This became a source of conflict between her and her husband, who had expected her to bring a large dowry to the marriage, fulfil household duties and be stimulating company. She had tried to loosen the ties with her father in order to gain her independence and to improve relations with her husband; in a bid for economic independence she had opened her own shop in the Meena Bazaar. Her brother, who had been given affection and education in large amounts, was now a millionaire, but did not consider it his responsibility to look after his father and the rest of the family. Instead it was still expected of her, despite her lack of education and opportunities. She was quite clear that if a woman was unable to find strength within herself, her children were likely to be adversely affected.

The woman in question was skilled at managing money, and had won the trust of her husband for her ability to handle finance. When, some nine years previously, the offer had arisen to buy a shop in the Meena Bazaar, her husband agreed for her to use her *mahir* (that part of the dowry which the husband provides for his wife) to finance the purchase. Her efforts in the shop had proved very lucrative and enabled her husband to buy more land and property. In her view, this proved that men wanted women only to bear children and to create wealth which they could show off to the world; they were never going to give women public credit for their talents. She was equally outspoken about the mullahs who, she said, behaved as if

Islam had just been invented. The position of men in society and the role of some of the mullahs made her even more determined to allow her daughter every possible opportunity. A good education, she felt, would equip her daughter with the skills to advance in her career and compete in a patriarchal society in which men sought to dominate women. She said, 'Man is responsible for the friction between women, i.e. mother and wife. Man is incapable of keeping both happy. He is responsible for the mistrust between women'. The politicisation that she displayed about gender relations was a result of her own experiences rather than a political ideology. She had clearly thought through the general implications of her own situation and rather than acting as a passive recipient in accepting her lot in life, she took active steps to challenge the status quo and particularly to ensure better chances for her daughter. As so often, there was a mismatch between effort and outcome and the mother's attempts were not necessarily to the satisfaction of the daughter.

Another woman, highly educated at a public school, had been encouraged by her family to excel in her education and her teachers had been keen for the girls to do well in the public school examinations, because their success added to the reputation of the school. She had been expected to contribute to the housework, but there had been no pressure on her to do so. Her father thought that it was more important for her than even her brother to gain an education, because of the additional responsibilities placed on women when they marry. Men could pursue their education after marriage. There were some problems at home, but she was working for both interest and financial independence.

The daughter of the owner of a shop selling women's garments was still pursuing a part-time BA degree. Her ambition was to specialise in commerce, so she was studying maths. Her maths results had always been spectacularly good. She had attended a co-educational school, and felt that this had been of great benefit to her: she was used to treating men like people. Her parents had always encouraged her to follow her own interests and abilities. Housework was on a rota basis, and her brother was responsible for the shopping. Although she was not given a wage for working at the shop, all her expenses were paid and she enjoyed the work, which kept her busy. She hoped to pursue a career after she married.

Another woman, the eldest of ten children, felt that she had been restricted in her choice of career because of her gender. Working in a shop allowed her the flexibility to pursue part-time studies, as well as working in an interesting and 'safe' environment. She was under pressure from her parents to marry and give up the shop, but she held out and kept control of her own money.

In another woman's family, the boys had to share responsibility for the housework. She had been educated up to age fourteen in a co-educational school, then in a single-sex school. She had gained BA and Master of Business Administration degrees. The shop in which she worked was a family business involving all the female members of the family.

A working-class woman was running a canteen in a shop she was renting; she was responsible for all the buying and the cooking. She had four children; her husband was a poorly-paid caretaker in a school, but with accommodation supplied as part of his job. He was one of the rare husbands who took major responsibility for the housework. Her canteen became profitable after a slow start, and enabled her to finance the family and pay for the education and other financial needs of the children. She controlled all the family income, including that of her husband, and made all the family decisions.

A woman who had worked as a teacher in Kuwait ran a cosmetics and ladies' lingerie shop. Her parents had always wanted her to have a good education, a priority in her family, and she had gained a BA. Pakistanis who live and work in Africa and the Middle East frequently send their children, especially daughters, to Pakistan for higher education. Some wealthy families may want both sons and daughters to be educated in the West; others send their sons to the West and their daughters to Pakistan. Yet others may send both to Pakistan. The former may indicate the order of priority given to men's and women's education, but still suggests that education for women is considered important. Another reason for choosing Pakistan could be that their daughters could stay with members of the extended family whilst training or working, as with the woman in question. Her home background freed her to concentrate on her studies and her career. Housework was the responsibility of the servants. She could be classed as a career woman since she was still unmarried at the age of forty. She lived with her grandmother, because her parents were still in Kuwait. As the eldest of four children, she took charge of the family's budget.

Another woman whose father had emigrated to Burma in search of work, had been forced to work to support the family without any financial assistance from her father. From the age of twelve she had begun to sew at home to make ends meet, and had begun her present work some twelve years earlier, continuing through marriage and widowhood. She owned the beauty parlour where she worked, employed ten women and kept control of her money. Through practical necessity, she had acquired the business acumen and confidence to own and run a lucrative business of which she was proud. One of her employees from a broken family, who wanted to be a doctor, said of her work as a beautician, 'It started as a hobby, but translated into a practical necessity'. She had been trained in macramé and flower arranging before training as a beautician. There was clearly a considerable gap between her stated ambition to be a doctor and her achievement as a beautician. Large sums of money are required for training in medicine, which her mother could not afford after her divorce. As in Britain, divorce takes its toll on the finances of the family and this can in turn affect children's educational outcomes.

The substance of the interviews is summarised in Table I. For each woman is shown her age; the educational level attained; her work or educational aspirations; the outcome of these to date, whether she owns her own shop and keeps her income; and what aspirations her parents had had for her. The table is set out in order of ascending age.

Most women had not realised their aspirations. Four wanted to be doctors, two teachers; one hoped to specialise in commerce, another to be a business administrator. Others were interested in part-time study while they worked. Some women's aspirations were in tune with their parents' whereas others' conflicted.

In Table II the women's aspirations are listed in rows, and compared with the parents' views on their daughters' futures. It can be seen that the two women who wanted to go into business were generally encouraged by their parents. This was probably instrumental in their success in retail business. But for women with other aspirations, there was a range of parental influences that extended from discouragement of work in general to active support of their chosen career.

Even when there was a clear relationship between parental and filial expectations, however, daughters did not always attain their full potential. The reasons varied: there was often a mismatch between the theoretical ideal and financial constraints; their brothers' needs received priority, or practical support was not given. For example the daughter of one of the shop-owners wanted to be a doctor and her mother concurred but the household responsibilities she had to assume were incompatible with the single-mindedness required for a medical course. The daughter thought she would have been a good doctor but she had had to sacrifice her chances to support her siblings; although still in education, she was also working in her mother's shop. Her personal needs were met, but she was not paid wages. She told me that despite her mother's frustration at having her own educational potential thwarted by her father and her determination to provide equality of opportunity for her children of both sexes, she treated her sons and daughters differentially. She said: 'No one is ever totally fair. That has always been and will be the case'. This is the daughter of the woman who was most outspoken about men. The force of societal expectation is such that women, almost in spite of themselves, to some degree repeat the familiar behaviour pattern and reproduce gender relations in each generation.

Many women came from middle-class backgrounds yet were unable to afford the education they most desired, and were pressured to support the family. They were, however, often in a position to choose where to work to gain financial independence, contribute towards their education, or simply avoid boredom. One, who was still studying part time, said, 'I got bored with sitting at home, so I thought of doing something. If it wasn't to be a doctor, then at least a beautician'. The flexibility of working at the Meena Bazaar enabled them to pursue their studies part time and have the satisfaction of financing themselves and the support of other women in the

**Table I: Aspirations of women working in Meena Bazaar**

| No | Age | Education | Aspirations | Outcome | Own shop | Keeps income | Parents' aspirations |
|---|---|---|---|---|---|---|---|
| 1 | 18 | Matric | Wanted to pursue education | Ended up working and doing dress-making course | ✗ | ✗ To family but keeps some for herself | Brother encouraged her to do beautician's |
| 2 | 19 | ? | MBA | Still studying | ✗ Family's | ✗ To family | Left to follow her own interests. No favouritism between boys and girls. |
| 3 | late teens | Matric | No idea – knew wouldn't get much education | Pleased with what she's achieved | ✗ | ✓ | ? |
| 4 | late teens early 20s | ? | Wanted financial independence | No financial independence but still studying | ✗ | ✗ To family | Both parents encourage education |
| 5 | early 20s | Studying for BA | No clear ideas – except college | Studying part-time | ✗ | ✓ | ? become rich |
| 6 | mid 20s | ? | Be a doctor | No practical support for her to study | ✗ Mother's | ✗ To family | Wanted her to be a doctor |
| 7 | mid 20s | To intermediate | Be a teacher | Financial pressures dictated she got job | ✗ Rented | ✓ | Want her to give up shop and get married |
| 8 | mid 20s | Intermediate | Be a doctor | Parents said no need to work so no study until beautician training | ✗ | ✓ | Father did not want her to work outside home |
| 9 | 20s | Studying for BA | Go into commerce | Still studying | ✗ Family's | ✗ To mother | Encourage to follow own interests |
| 10 | 27 | Intermediate | Be a doctor | Mother died – had to get job | ✗ | ✓ Not married | Parents encouraged education but boys got priority |
| 11 | 36 | Matric and beautician's course | Be a doctor | Couldn't be doctor because of financial problems | ✗ | ✓ | ? |

**Table I: Aspirations of women working in Meena Bazaar (continued)**

| No | Age | Education | Aspirations | Outcome | Own shop | Keeps income | Parents' aspirations |
|----|-----|-----------|-------------|---------|----------|--------------|----------------------|
| 12 | 40 | BA | Be a teacher | Did this before opening shop | ✓ Family bought it | ✗ Not married | Encouraged to pursue education |
| 13 | 40 | Elementary | Did not think about job | Husband died – had to get job | ✓ | ✓ | ? Education not possible because father didn't send money |
| 14 | mid 40s | Matric | ? Saved 15 years for shop | Bought shop | ✓ | ✓ with struggle | Low – different expectations for boys and girls |
| 15 | late 40s | Elementary | Pursue education. But running business | Financial constraints met | ✗ Rented | ✓ and husband's | ? |

**Notes on Table I**

Elementary education – primary school education (normally up to age 11)
Matric (Matriculation) – certificate in secondary education (up to age 16)
Intermediate – 2-year course entrance exam for university

| ✗ | = | no |
|---|---|-----|
| ✓ | = | yes |
| ? | = | question not asked, or no clear answer |

**Table II: Relation between parents' and daughter's aspirations**

| Apiration | Education encouraged | Difference between boys and girls | Wanted same as daughter | Encourage generally | Discourage from work |
|-----------|---------------------|-----------------------------------|-------------------------|---------------------|----------------------|
| Shop | | 14 | | | |
| Doctor | 10 | 10 | 6 | | 8 |
| Studying Commerce/ Business | | | | 2, 9 | |
| Teacher | 12 | | | | 7 |
| No idea | | 13 | | | |

The numbers refer to the individuals listed in Table 1.

complex, whose presence lent strength to their cause, overtly and in subtle ways. The sheer presence of women on certain courses and career paths encouraged others to follow. Only two women were compelled to work because of through a desperate financial reasons – in the one case the husband's death.

The women were generally far more critical of men in general and their husbands in particular than they were of their fathers. Only one woman claimed that her brother had been educated at her expense and that her father had tried to instil into her a sense of inferiority. Her mother had died when she was still a child and she was subjected to mental and physical abuse from her husband.

Often women's educational advancement was hampered for financial reasons even when they were supported by all the family including the men. For example, one woman who wanted to be a doctor lived with her divorced mother who was financially dependent upon her brother, who could not afford to support his niece through a medical course. Another woman who also wanted to be a doctor could not study because the family's financial situation required her to work. The women who felt particularly thwarted in their careers were those who wanted to be doctors, for which training all over the world is long and expensive and so only in the reach of a few.

Table III shows that women who were studying or wanting to go into commerce did not own their own shops. They tended to see working in Meena Bazaar as a temporary measure, as a stepping-stone or as a way to finance their studies. Women with other aspirations had come to terms with the idea that these would not be met, and working in Meena Bazaar was now their main career aim.

Table IV shows a spread of aspirations for different ages. The younger women tended to have a greater interest in education than older women had had at their age. This may reflect a general change in attitude towards education after Independence. Independence of the Subcontinent and the coincidental partition of India and Pakistan broke up traditional families and communities. Land and property,

| Table III: Shop ownership of women working at Meena Bazaar | | | |
|---|---|---|---|
| **Aspiration** | **Own Shop** | **Family's/Rented Shop** | **Work in Shop** |
| Shop | 1 | | |
| Doctor | 1 | 1 | 2 |
| Studying | | 1 | 3 |
| Commerce/Business | | 2 | |
| Teacher | 1 | 1 | |
| No idea | 1 | | 1 |

**Table IV: Relation between Aspirations and Age**

| Apiration | Under 20 | 20 – 30 | 30 – 40+ |
|---|---|---|---|
| Shop | | | 1 |
| Doctor | | 2 | |
| Studying | 2 | 1 | |
| Commerce/Business | 1 | 1 | |
| Teacher | 1 | | 1 |
| No idea | 1 | | 1 |

which had been important status symbols were left behind, so could no longer be the main indicators of social standing. Other factors such as education became more important. Education for women had been a integral part of the struggle against British colonialism and grew in importance with the change to a more urbanised economy. It has become accepted for 'respectable' middle-class women to earn money and what matters now is the type of occupation they follow. By and large, professional careers requiring education and training are considered acceptable. Working-class women in the Subcontinent, as elsewhere, never had any choice in the matter. They have always been driven by the force of financial circumstances to undertake paid work, ranging from construction to mining. They could not afford the luxuries of purdah or of an education.

## Banking and insurance

Banking and insurance companies have very hierarchical structures, based primarily on academic qualifications and professional training. In-service training generally takes place away from home. This can limit women's progress in these organisations, as domestic constraints are more likely to prevent them from taking advantage of it. Further, married women are more likely to support their husbands' careers, missing the chance of their own promotion. Additionally, women often experience direct discrimination in the workplace. Once a tradition is established it is difficult to break, and pioneering women all over the world are subjected to sexual harassment which degrades and undermines their efforts as professional women in, for instance, the police force or politics. Women in Britain have similar experiences and so do women in banking in the United States of America.

In both Britain and America women are still primarily concentrated in the lower echelons of professional management. Estimated figures show that between 50 and 20 per cent of entry-level managers are women; 5 per cent middle management; only 1 per cent executive. This is despite Equal Opportunities legislation. The 1986 Industrial Society survey paints a picture which has universal validity. Both social and structural constraints affect women's aspirations in these professions.

Of the sample 74 per cent said that it was important for them to have opportunities for promotion, and only 37 per cent felt that they had the same opportunities as the men. Many women have high aspirations but are aware of structural constraints.

### Interviews

The women in these professions interviewed in Mysore and Bangalore in India seemed to be in typical situations. An economic researcher at a Bombay bank said, 'I always wanted to be successful, have power; I wanted to work'. She said that training for banking often involves staying away overnight and this was one of the major factors in women not achieving equality with their male colleagues. This was in addition to the general discrimination against women, particularly those who are married. Married women are assumed to subordinate their career aspirations to those of their husbands. The researcher, however, continued to secure her rightful place in training and promotion, which often resulted in covert sexist comments from her male colleagues. Her family also came under pressure from the community at large for not getting her married off because she earned good money. The success of a young unmarried woman in career terms also has to be seen in relation to its other social implications. In the Subcontinent there is a general view that it is not 'honourable' for parents to call on their daughters' earnings. Parents are expected to be responsible for the welfare of their daughters and if daughters do earn, the money should be for their personal use or part of their dowry. This is one significant reason why families forbid their daughters to undertake paid work. When women do work because of financial necessity or out of interest, their contribution is often minimised and their income spent on non-essentials.

However, not all the women interviewed had high initial aspirations or were aware of the full constraints on realising them. Two women told me they had no idea what they wanted to do and both said this was because they were not expected to work after marriage.

One woman came into banking through family connections at a time (1962) when the male manager was keen to recruit women to set up an all-women branch. At the time of the interview this branch employed 75 staff, all of them women except for two errand boys and a caretaker. The woman manager of the branch said that she felt a sense of achievement 'when other women come to me with their personal and financial problems, for example, opening up bank accounts without their husbands' knowledge'. Before her present post she had for seven years had an administrative post in charge of planning. She held a Master's degree in Economics from Madras University, and her ambition had been to be a lecturer. Since this involved time away from home, her mother was not keen. She had reconsidered her career plans accordingly and applied for a job in the local branch of the bank of which she became the manager. Whilst she had clearly benefited from a single-sex banking system in terms of her career and as a role model for other women, she nonetheless advocated co-education which, she felt, would make women less self-conscious in their working environment. This was a view supported by the women in Meena Bazaar who had experienced co-education. This woman was particularly interesting as her career success and independence did not translate itself to the domestic arena. Prior to her marriage she handed over her money to her widowed mother who had to support her thirteen younger siblings. After marriage, her husband made all the household decisions: 'I am a manager only in the bank. Like Hamlet, you don't have to ask the question, to be or not to be'. She appeared to be happy to assume different roles according to circumstances and highlighted the dangers of drawing hasty conclusions from any situation. Her case provides further evidence that women-only workplaces can encourage other women, by providing both an employment role model and appropriate service delivery.

I interviewed an architect, a homeopathy student and a worker in a women's bookshop to see if they exemplified possible wide-spread middle-class aspirations and constraints. The architect said that this was what she had wanted to be for as long as she could remember, but she was facing difficulties within her profession, as men usually assumed the role of assessing new sites and meeting new clients on grounds that it gave a better impression. She said, 'In Parsi families there is more equality between the sexes, but my father keeps charge of the finances'. Not only had she been interested in gaining a good education but she had also received considerable encouragement from her family. She was about to go abroad to obtain a higher degree. It is instructive to note that she somehow did not connect the control of income by her father as a breach of equality between the sexes – rather like a Western woman describing her husband as being 'rather good because he does the washing up.'

Except for one Parsi and one Christian all the women interviewed were Hindus. The constraints on women and their achievements varied according to the class position of the family and particular circumstances rather than their religious background. The similarity between their situation and that of the Muslim women interviewed in Karachi does not sustain the commonly held view that Muslim women necessarily live in a more rigid hierarchical society and have fewer chances of education and employment than women of other faiths.

The homeopathy student had trained in Bailgam; for further training she would need to go to Calcutta, which had the most prestigious homeopathy teaching course. If she married, her husband and his family would determine whether or not she would practise her profession. She commented that 'In Indian society, the emphasis is on the mother bringing up the children herself, which she can't do if she works'. The equality of earning power between husband and wife was not really an issue. 'The girl herself accepts a different role in life before and after marriage'.

She accepted that poor people had to work, but for people of her class, it did not matter if they did not work after they had their education. Girls were not expected to do housework while they were studying, but accepted it as part of their duties after marriage. Such acquiescence obviously limits women's progress in a hierarchical structure.

A new feminist bookshop in Bangalore run by a divorced Christian woman had been started by a women's rights theatre group seeking to mobilise public opinion. Lack of funds had hampered their ambition to make films, but they were working with media writers and reviewers to obtain films on women from all over the world. They had managed to bring together Indian women artists to display some work on rape. They were also working with women on combating the problem of domestic violence. The bookshop manager was one of the most politicised women I interviewed. She was actively involved in campaigning against domestic violence and polygyny. She wanted to raise the status of divorced women. She felt that her Christian community held the same negative views about divorcées as the Hindu majority amongst whom they lived. (None of the divorced women in Pakistan discussed this social phenomenon or attitudes towards it, so no comparisons are possible.)

Commenting on a bigamous case, she said that there was great pressure from society on women to conform and not to separate or go to court. In one case of bigamy, the husband had begged his wife not to go to court; when she returned to the house her husband, a doctor, slowly poisoned her. The husband could not be committed due to lack of evidence, but the women's group had achieved a small victory in that the matrimonial home had been divided so that three-fourths was allocated to the children of the marriage, and only one part to the husband.

The next woman interviewed was so successful in the insurance world that she had purchased an entire island of coconut groves off the Mysore coast. She had started work comparatively late, after her husband had lost a good job and she needed an income to pay for the private education of their children. Her job caused considerable friction with her in-laws, with whom they had lived; the problem was resolved by the in-laws moving out.

## Education

The aspirations of teachers both in the Subcontinent and in the West indicate the role of education in preparing women for their place in society. Gender differentiation in education was partly imported from Britain during the colonial era, and sustained by the needs of empire. This is summed up in the words of George Orwell:

> We teach young men to drink whisky and play football, I admit, but precious little else. Look at our schools – factories for cheap clerks. We've never taught a

single useful manual trade to the Indians. We daren't; frightened of competition in industry. We've even crushed various industries. Where are the Indian muslins now? Back in the 'forties or thereabouts they were building sea- going ships in India, and manning them as well. Now you couldn't build a sea-worthy fishing boat there. In the eighteenth century the Indians cast guns which were at any rate up to European standard. Now, after we've been in India for a hundred and fifty years, you can't make so much as a brass cartridge case in the whole continent. (Orwell, 1958)

After independence the education system was modelled on that of Britain. A Madras newspaper of 1885 noted:

(India's) need is to devise a system of education for Hindu females as will make her an agreeable companion, a good mother, an intelligent and loving wife, and an excellent housewife. We want her to possess those mental accomplishments which enable the wife to serve as a solace to her husband in his bright and dark moments, the mother to undertake or at least to supervise the early instruction of her child, and the lady of the house to provide those greatest social comforts idealised in the English woman's home (source unobtainable).

The history of education in the Subcontinent shows that attention was being paid to the education of women from an early period. The Mohammedan Education Congress of 1886 had turned its attention to women's education even before the establishment of a sound infrastructure. A separate women's teacher training college was established in Calcutta in 1899 and the slow progress in educating women began. Subba-Lakshi Ammal, a Brahmin widow, was the first to be trained as a teacher in her community, and she founded a widows' home in 1931 which later became a teacher training college.

The period between the turn of the century and 1947 is characterised by the growth of women's movements, organised by women involved in issues concerning their education, franchise and the nationalist movement. Hilary Standing (1975) comments that 'teaching is considered to be the most 'honourable' occupation for women.' She also notes that in women's occupational patterns in West Bengal, employment is restricted to the areas of teaching and clerical work, this latter being less desirable, but that 'there also emerged a tendency to play down the financial importance of women's earnings to the family budget'.

Education for women is not new to the Subcontinent. As we have seen, women in the Subcontinent have been writing and contributing to socio-political debate since 600 BC. This tradition of education for women applies in both Hindu and Muslim cultures. Prophet Muhammad said, 'Seek knowledge even if it means going to China' (at the time considered to be a place of knowledge and enlightenment). Ironically, the religion whose prophet had sought to promote education even beyond national boundaries was used to deny women access to education in India during the British Raj by denouncing as heretical the learning of English and Western-style education. Most of the education for worldly success was in English and on the Western model, so Muslims, and in particular women, were increasingly isolated from worldly success and left in ignorance. In certain quarters, Islam is still being used to deny women their rightful place in society, including access to education and employment opportunities. The question for women in the Subcontinent, as everywhere else, remains: to what use is education put? Is it for the self-realisation of women, to enable them to have control over their lives, or is it to become another commodity to be shown off to others – little more than a status symbol? So instead of being merely a pretty wife she is now also expected to be educated; but this takes her no further in the true sharing of power, whether domestic, economic or political.

Standing (1975) observes that 'In India, for instance, married women may be confined to a very few occupational categories because of prevailing norms of family respectability to which they are crucially subject, and also by notions of what constitutes suitable work for women'. This could be seen as merely a 'safety valve' in a patriarchal society, allowing women access to a limited number of jobs, which are considered 'respectable'. It allows women some freedom to exercise their intellect, earn income which they may or may not control, be free of household responsibilities for at least the period they are away from home and widen their circle of social contacts. It also gives them pride and a sense of achievement over and above the monetary gains. This situation, however, may restrict them to a comfort zone out of which they may find it difficult to venture and compete with men.

An interview with Shameen Khazi, a marketing consultant, social worker and regional councillor, bears this out (Karachi: *Daily Gang*, December 23 1987). She referred to the time when few women in the Subcontinent worked outside the home. Gradually their number had grown, but it was still small and confined mainly to teaching and medicine. These areas of employment showed not only a traditional pattern but yet another manifestation of male selfishness and dominance. 'It is because men want their women to be educated and treated by women'.

## Aspirations of teachers

Only three out of the 14 women interviewed had wanted to be teachers as their first choice. One in her mid-30s was one of five sisters and had longed to work in a bank, but had been unable to get employment without the right connections and her gender might not have helped. She had responsibility for the household duties, which conflicted with the 9am-5pm working day at a bank; teaching offered a more congenial arrangement. She was not the only woman to choose teaching because of its working hours and holidays, which were more compatible with child care and running a home. Women in the West choose teaching as a career for similar reasons, as the main responsibility of child care still rests with women.

Some of the women were given the same chances as their brothers in education. One woman said that her father was keener for his daughters to be educated and skilled before marriage than his sons because men could always continue their education after they marry, but women have to take on domestic responsibilities. Because of women's socialisation their account of equal treatment between the sexes is based on their unequal expectations. One said that there was no difference in educational aspirations between sisters and brother and then said, 'because there was only one boy, he got priority'. Despite the history of concern for separate educational treatment for women, the curricular structure was the same for girls and boys at school and they sat the same public examinations.

When women are interviewed, they tend to exaggerate gender equality at work. Anna Pollert (1981) found that women in a tobacco factory in Bristol boasted about how they shared the housework with their husbands but closer questioning revealed that the men did very little. What women say about such matters is not necessarily objective but is skewed by their expectation of getting very unequal treatment.

Some of the women had problems maintaining their careers. One of the Pakistani women who had been teaching for eighteen years found that when she married, her being at work for twelve hours a day caused conflict. She did not succumb to pressure because too much was at stake. She regarded marriage as, 'a necessary social evil'. She took girls on camping trips and involved them in practical agricultural training all over Pakistan. Before her marriage, she took secondary age girls on trips for several weeks at a time and yet teachers in Britain often cannot take their Asian women students out for so much as an evening at the theatre. Do the parents have more confidence in the particular teacher or in the education system itself?

Another woman, now a head teacher, had struggled with her family, particularly her grandmother, to be allowed to become a teacher. Her grandmother saw no reason for women to have higher education and thought it was 'not respectable' to earn money; it was men's responsibility to support the family. Before this teacher married she handed all her earnings to her mother, who managed the household budget; but after marriage she kept her income and her husband's and they jointly decided to spend her money for the children's education, and her husband's to run the house. 'His job is to earn, and mine is to run the household – simple matter,' was her summing up.

One woman followed her sister into teaching. All the women in her family were educated and there was equal emphasis on higher education for both sexes. She kept all her earnings for herself until her father died, when she contributed a little to support the family budget, but most was provided by one of her brothers. After she married she had kept control of her own income and used money from her husband to run the house.

Another woman had trained as a teacher after her degree, seeing it only as a useful interim measure but remained in the profession for fifteen years once her interest was kindled. She was unmarried and kept control of all her income, sometimes giving a little to her family.

One head teacher observed that: 'When I was training there was not enough careers guidance; now there is much better information on career choices which means that women are choosing engineering as a possible career.' Sharifa Khama, a pioneering woman airline pilot in Pakistan who opened a school for women to train as pilots a decade ago, has been an inspiration for women in that field – a model that could be emulated in the West.

Despite the respectability of the profession it is not always easy for women to become teachers. It depends on whether the family accept that women should earn money – the equivalent of the West's: 'I can support my wife: she doesn't need to work'. Women needed encouragement and support from their families while studying – and freedom from domestic chores. This is in direct contrast to the stereotype of Asian women in the West, as chained to the kitchen sink and not allowed to study. For example, in *Pakistani Wives in Britain* it is stated: 'Their lives are limited to the kitchen, the children and religious rituals' (Parmar, 1982). For another teacher, the domestic chores expected of her made it harder to do well in examinations, but she had still succeeded. Unmarried, she supported her family. Her father had died and her mother was handicapped; it was her money that was putting her sisters through their education.

Another unmarried woman, in her fifties, had been teaching for thirty years. Contrary to stereotypes in the West there is a long tradition of Asian women not marrying but choosing to devote themselves to pursuits of the mind; Buddhist nuns are examples of this. This interviewee had no domestic responsibilities; all her needs were met by members of her brother's family with whom she lived. She controlled her own income and gave whatever she considered reasonable towards the household costs – even less than previously, as all her brother's children had now become independent. Her younger sister was responsible for the actual running of the household.

Once women had entered the profession, it was possible for them to fulfil their career aspirations. It was surprising to note that the Director of Education in Karachi was a woman, as were many of school inspectors. Men only featured on the third tier down in the hierarchy, as administrators. This woman's entry into the profession had been almost entirely due to pressure from her father, rather against her own inclination. After a BA and a Certificate in Education as a secondary teacher, she used to visit the private school operated by her brother, so acquiring some experience, but she had little interest in teaching. Nevertheless, she felt obliged to take up the headship offered to her when her brother's school, along with other private schools, was nationalised in the 1970s. She had married, and controlled both her own and her husband's income, making all the decisions on expenditure. Her husband would get the children ready for school and do the shopping, but she insisted on cooking and cleaning the house herself – perhaps because she did not approve of his efforts in this direction or because she identified with the roles most directly associated with her status as a woman.

The mother of another woman had been against her going to college, because college 'spoiled girls'. To her original Matriculation she had added a teacher training qualification and she now had a job in a primary school. To teach at secondary level she would need a degree. Her father wanted her to have higher education but was not in a position to support her in her aspiration and all her income was being saved towards a dowry.

The marriage of one woman had taken place during her teacher training, and this made it hard for her to complete it. But she succeeded – only to be beset by the problem of finding employment. Her first post was as a temporary replacement for another teacher on leave. She subsequently secured a permanent contract. All her income, indeed all the income of the family, was handed over to her mother-in-law, whose word in the house was law. 'She's the head of the household. No-one else counts, including father-in-law'.

The teachers came from middle to lower middle-class backgrounds, whereas the Meena Bazaar women were from a wider social spectrum and with few easily marketable skills. It is more of a conscious decision to become a teacher and far more difficult to save money for a four-year BA and a year's B.Ed. than to serve in a shop and save money to start a retail shop.

## Manufacturing

The experience of women working in a clothing factory in Karachi was entirely different. Eight out of the 15 were widows, two had fathers who were terminally ill, four others had domestic problems. These problems were cited as reasons for work. There was only one for whom financial need was not the primary reason for entering employment; ironically, she was an accountant.

The supervisor had wanted to be a teacher, but her father's death prevented it. The company for which she worked made men's clothing for export to Japan and she had had relevant experience. Her own difficult financial circumstances made her sympathetic to the needs of others who had little or no family or financial support.

She tried to recruit and train women who really needed the work, for example teenagers who had lost their fathers, or widows with children. Before she became a supervisor, there were no women employed in the company as machinists, on grounds that women would be unwilling to work there. To this she had retorted 'If women can't work here, then every other door is also shut to them. What will then happen to the orphans and widows?' She negotiated with the male management to employ women who had little or no employment opportunities and guaranteed that the work would be up to standard.

She emphasised to these women machinists that they must be punctual and achieve a high professional standard. The work was done on a contractual basis, although only men had been given contracts in the past. In contrast to working in the Meena Bazaar or teaching, which were seen as relatively attractive activities, working in a factory was a matter of necessity. The women who were interested in their work were not machinists but the accountant, a supervisor and an assistant supervisor. Few talked about their parents' aspirations for them, which were overshadowed by the reality of having to earn a living.

One woman with three children was a refugee from Bangladesh who had come to Karachi in 1974 after her husband was killed in the war between East and West Pakistan. She had never worked before and had only an elementary education.

An emigrant from Bangladesh had been suddenly widowed and sought work in Pakistan to support her six sons. She had been in the factory for four years and was one of the few women with a formal training in sewing, received at a technical school in Bangladesh. All six of her sons were in education, and although she took responsibility for the domestic duties, she expected her sons to wash up and cook occasionally.

The accountant, who had recently emigrated from India, complained of poor employment opportunities in India: 'The best you could hope for was teaching'. In Pakistan she could have worked in a government department or a bank, but would have needed further training as the Indian system was slightly different so she settled for the post with the garment manufacturer. Her father was a local government officer, still resident in India, who intended joining the rest of the family in Pakistan on retirement. The eldest of ten children, she was supporting the entire family with the help of two of her sisters.

Most machinists did not appear much interested in their job but had no desire to do anything else. As one woman said, 'Who doesn't like being at home? Because of financial compulsion you have to go out to work'.

One of the older women, a widow with two children to support, had been working in the factory for four years, and had eighteen years' experience of machining garments in different factories. She allowed her son to control the family income, as she thought him a better manager of money. She found life in this factory more ful-filling than elsewhere because machinists were responsible for the entire garment, and felt able to concentrate away from the domestic environment.

The death of a male member of family was crucial in women going out to work. One cannot necessarily assume that the women in the factory were all from work-ing-class backgrounds. Many of the machinists had come from Bangladesh (formerly East Pakistan) and their social status has no direct equivalent in the social structure in Pakistan. All the women employed in other jobs had education at least up to matriculation, plus professional training. Thirteen of the machinists had pro-fessional training in clothing technology. Others had learnt 'on the job'. Two women were trained machinists, but did not work as machinists until after their husbands died. It was not clear whether women who were machinists could aspire to, for example, a supervisor's post.

The professional standards demanded were rewarded with good wages. However, support from the family was also important. Many women had to be courageous and enterprising to venture out to work, often with young children and little training but socialised for the responsibility of earning a living.

The economic circumstances and family dynamics even within this small group are diverse. Some of the women had complete control of family finances, even before they became economically active. Others, although working, handed their earnings over to other members of the family whom they considered to be better managers of money than themselves. The level of professional skill shown by the women was impressive, and had in most cases been gained through on-the-job training.

The myth that Asian women are invariably dependent on their men for economic control and family decision-making was not supported among even this working-class group. They worked because they had to and they took their own decisions. They were an economically independent, realistic and clear-thinking group, who had, with their supervisor, deliberately created a women-friendly workplace which provided job satisfaction and a regular and reasonable income.

## Comparison with Britain

Britain is an industrial nation with a mixed economy. Politically, it is classed as a liberal democracy. It is patriarchal and socially stratified. The last four hundred years of its colonial history contributed to its wealth and to the notion of racial and cultural superiority. It was comparatively easy for Britain to rely upon its former colonies to supply it with markets for its goods and cheap labour after the Second World War. The ideology and practice of racism in its personal and institutional forms affects the life chances of Asians living in Britain and has created the general context of the position of Asian women in British society. However, Asian working women also have to be considered in the context of the overall position of working women in Britain. By 1980 the number of working women had risen to 9 million as opposed to 13 million men. 'Almost two million women work in occupations that are almost entirely (over 90 per cent) done by women – typists, secretaries, maids, nurses, canteen assistants, sewing machinists' (Parmar, 1982).

The position of Asian women in Britain is further complicated by a recurring situation where Asian girls are given different careers advice to that of their white counterparts, on the assumption that they would be forced into an early arranged marriage. In Britain, Asian women tend to be confined to specific jobs dependent upon regional variations. They are concentrated in low-paid and unskilled or semi-skilled jobs: as machinists in the clothing industry, in laundries, light engineering, as cleaners and home workers. According to *Labour Market Trends*, there were 382,000 employees working in the manufacture of clothing, textiles, leather and leather products in 1995 (*Government Statistical Service*, 1995). Of these, 18,200 females were working full-time in the manufacture of made-up textile articles, and 3,600 part-time. A further 98,400 were working full-time in the manufacture of wearing apparel, and 17,600 part-time. The average gross weekly earnings of full-time female workers was £169 per week, which works out at £4.11 per hour.

One of the areas of employment in Britain, as in the Subcontinent, is in garment manufacturing, either in clothing factories (or sweatshops) or from home. As businesses have declined and competition increased, Asian women have looked for other channels. Recently, co-operatives and small businesses have been set up with community support, to use existing skills within the community and to offer an alternative to home working for women. One clothing business, producing school uniforms for Asian girls, was set up by a community development worker with the Methodist Church, with some funding from Birmingham City Council and the East Birmingham Task Force. An essential feature is the provision of a créche and of flexible working hours. It is also an all-women workplace.

Batley City Challenge has a co-operative to train workers to produce one-off garments for private customers. A selection of *shalwar qumeez*, dresses, trousers and suits, made from the customers' own fabric, as well as sample garments to show to dress shops and boutiques, are made in this women-only workplace, which also offers flexible hours. Allen and Wolkowitz (1987) describe how members of ethnic minorities, who suffer high rates of unemployment, may be forced to set up as sub-contractors employing members of their own communities as home workers.

It is wrong to assume that 'ethnic minority' women are prevented from working outside the home for cultural reasons. These women work for much the same reasons as their white counterparts, namely for economic reasons. They supplement the family income and additionally gain freedom from the isolation of house-work. 'It is often believed that home workers from ethnic minorities choose this form of work because of cultural disapproval of work outside the home, a lack of English language skills or the fear of racial harassment' (National Group on Home Working, 1994). The NGHW study interviewed 175 home workers over a two-year period beginning in 1991 in Leeds, Rochdale, Oldham, London, Nottingham, Birmingham, Manchester, Leicester, Wakefield and Calderdale, and is one of the broadest surveys of home working yet carried out in Britain.

Most home workers are working for the clothing and textile-related industries, and this is even more marked for the Asian home workers, 81 per cent of whom do this type of work and 97 per cent of whom do sewing. 'It seems likely that discrimination in the outside labour market plays a major role in limiting the choices open to Asian women, thus producing a concentration in home working. This is consistent with the finding... that Asian home workers are more likely than their white counterparts to state a preference for working outside the home, given a free choice' (NGHW, 1994, *ibid.*).

Only 15 per cent of all the home workers interviewed said that their households would experience no financial hardship if they gave up work and 53 per cent said that they would suffer severe hardship. The reasons for working from home are, again, exactly the same as those for the majority population. Although there were some Asian women who cited language reasons, fear of racism or family dis-approval of their working outside the home, they were outnumbered by those who did not cite these reasons. '...the reasons for home working are primarily structural, rather than cultural, with the need to care for children in the home constituting by far the most important of these reasons' (NGHW, 1994).

The other myth was also not borne out by the sample: no-one was employed by her relatives and over half worked for white managers. Whilst three interviewees said they were fearful of going out, others had worked outside the home before starting homework.

Women home workers have various skills which are not really valued. They seldom gain jobs as skilled as those they had before leaving to have children. Ballard (1984) and Coyle (1984), quoted in *Home Working* (Allen and Wolkowitz, 1987) substantiate the argument that women work for financial reasons and these do not disappear with marriage.

The National Group on Home Working's Briefing Paper No. 9 'Home Working: Women and Race' examines the particular characteristics of black women home workers are examined. 'Their range of jobs seems to be more limited than white women's. In particular a study in Coventry highlighted how in their sample only white women were doing clerical homework, whilst all the Asian women were doing sewing and packing homework' (NGHW, 1994). The black women had fewer employment rights than white women, and greater job insecurity. Their working hours were longer, and their rates of pay were below average. According to two reports produced in 1994 by the Equal Opportunities Commission, even when black and ethnic minority women were skilled and experienced they were still twice as likely to be unemployed or work longer hours in poor conditions and for lower pay than white women (Bhavan, 1994, Owen, 1994, quoted in NGHW Briefing Paper No 9).

Kosack (1975) indicates how immigrant women are oppressed in a number of ways. They are often wage slaves, either directly or through their husband's work. They have no say in what is produced or how. They contribute by engaging in reproduction of the next generation of male labour. Their children, because of educational barriers, are subjected to the same limitations as the previous generation.

She quotes from Amrit Wilson's book *Finding a Voice* (1978) to illustrate Asian women's oppression by white women. Asian women are said to have

> ...low salaries and everything is worse for them, they have to face the insults of supervisors. Those supervisors are all English women. The trouble is that in Britain our women are expected to behave like servants and we are not used to behaving like servants and we can't. But if we behave normally the supervisors start shouting and harassing us – they complain about us Indians to the manager.

The experience of most Asians in the workplace, both in the professions and in manual work, is characterised by racial discrimination and differential pay. The latter is done in a variety of ways: in some instances Asian and white workers are paid different rates for the same job. In others, less favourable working conditions are given to – for example shift work, nights or jobs which are dangerous and which the white work force would consequently prefer not to do.

> There is a lot of discrimination. In fact discrimination has always been present ever since I started working here thirteen years ago on three shillings a week. We got differential pay rates from the white women working with us and harassment from the supervisors, who have always been white since my days at the factory (Carby, 1982).

Asian women in a sewing factory exploit a stereotype of themselves and their chums, using their difficulty in speaking English to their own advantage and as a form of resistance. For example they would ask for instructions to be given several times over, on the grounds of having poor English. This was a delaying tactic and if they made a mistake in the sewing that too was blamed on their poor English.

Despite very difficult working conditions and the weight of racism against them, Asian women in Britain have continued to play an important part in struggles for improvement. On 10 October 1980, Asian women went on strike at a bubble gum factory. They were subjected to oppressive and dirty working conditions and differential pay: 95p per hour for Asians and £1.10 per hour for whites. When a woman who was pregnant asked for lighter work she was refused and when she then lost the baby, all the Asian workers made their anger known.

Asian women have been at the forefront of numerous industrial, political and social struggles during the last two decades. They have also been subjected to the full oppressive force of industrial racism at all levels of British society (Parmar, 1982). Yet existing literature on Asian people in Britain has tended to categorise certain forms of behaviour and lifestyle as social aberrations.

It is ironic that Asian women in Britain should find themselves even more confined than their counterparts in the Indian Subcontinent when Britain is viewed as an economically and politically advanced society offering a wide range of opportunities for success. Carby quotes two 'Asian' schoolgirls:

> Many Asian girls strongly resent being stereotyped as weak, passive, quiet girls who would not dare to lift a finger in their own defence. They want to challenge the idea people have of them as girls who do not want to stand out or cause trouble but tip-toe about hoping nobody will notice them (Carby, 1982).

They resist and struggle both in the Subcontinent and in Britain, but their situation in Britain is more difficult because of racism and the lack of role models from their own racial and cultural group. A report by the Commission for Racial Equality in March 1988 on a survey of six local education authorities illustrates the small number of Asian women in the teaching profession. Those who are employed are concentrated primarily on the lower rungs of their professional ladder or in support services paid under Section 11 of the Local Government Act, 1966.

## Interviews with women in the Indian Subcontinent – control of income

In examining the control of income, a number of factors need to be borne in mind:

- liberation and the issue of control over earned income

- the right to work without control over finance

- non-earning women and control over the family budget

- the relationship between power and earned income

- Muslim women and their control over earned income

Leghorn and Parker (1981) argue that economics powerfully affects the lives of all, especially women. Women are not seen by most societies as producers of goods. It therefore follows that they deserve little remuneration. Economic decision-making is mystified and specialised, further undermining women's right to participate in the decision-making process, on the grounds for example that they can only carry out unspecialised work. Not only is the work unspecialised but the skills involved in it are devalued.

The whole economic system is sustained by those in power and translated in the social relations within the family – where women carry out household chores without payment under the mysterious notion of love for the family. Wives of even rich men can only be accepted if they continue to enact their prescribed role. Other family members, usually men, achieve at the expense of women. 'Since women do the least specialised, low-status work, they do not have the same access to the crucial resources that would enable them to wield more power within their families and their communities' (Leghorn and Parker, 1981). Further, they appear to have no control over the resources of their families and society in general.

Women's right to inherit land in Islam is complex, for though Islam permits women one-half of male land right, the practice of seclusion of women among wealthier households means that they cannot cultivate the land or directly negotiate market prices. Such things are done through male intermediaries. During British rule Muslim women lost these rights of inheritance and were only allowed to keep the land due to their minor sons, in keeping with Hindu customary law as described in Chapter 2).

To view control of income exclusively in terms of power over what is earned may not give the full picture. Some women control or have influence over the expenditure of income even when it is not earned by them. Conversely some women have earning power but little or no say on how it is spent.

> Much of the debate about the importance of waged work for women has been cast in terms of women's capacity to 'control' resources which accrue to them through their individual earning power or by virtue of their kinship status. Control is used here as a synonym for 'capacity to make decisions regarding their use', but used in this narrow sense, it cannot stand as a measure of increased 'personal' autonomy in the sense of an enhanced capacity to determine the conditions of their own lives (Standing, 1975).

The middle-class Western assumption that a woman's control over finance can be gained through paid work does not apply to the women who were interviewed. It is quite clear that earning income and having control over decisions are not the same and the two are not to be confused. The picture is much more complex than it at first appears; power within the family is not solely based on earning capacity, but this does not detract from the importance of women earning an income.

The tables show that older women were more likely to keep their income than younger ones. This indicates that older women have more power within the family than younger ones. However, control over earned income is only one part of the relationship between position in the household and earnings. The women who were immigrants from India may have felt isolated in the absence of the extended family network. So would those who were divorced and suffered social stigmatisation, and also the young women whose families could not support their pursuit of higher education, just like those of Meena Bazaar. Women in these situations would have different status within the household, which would affect whether they could keep their income and control household spending.

'In a traditional extended family network, it was usually the eldest women who wielded power. But the new technology values young women who can be employed at low wages, the result being to lower the status of older women' (Standing, 1975). Several assumptions are made here; firstly that older women do not work and secondly that younger working women will automatically increase their status within the family because of their income. Standing assumes that power within the family is based on who is earning, rather than on who has control over decision-making.

Although men's earnings are often insufficient to support the family, the notion of women being dependent upon them impedes women's struggle for similar remuneration.

Concerning the distribution of resources within the Bengali household, Standing (1975) notes that: '... there are compelling reasons to be sceptical of the extent to which waged employment *per se* automatically affects, or even more, improves, women's situation'. We have seen that women enter the labour force on different terms from men. They are bearers not simply of labour power but also of gender characteristics rooted in the asymmetrical relations of a prior sexual division of labour (Young, Wolkowitz and McCullagh, 1981). Standing (1975) observes that 'In India, for instance, married women may be confined to a very few occupational categories because of prevailing norms of family respectability to which they are crucially subject, and also what constitutes suitable work for women'. In essence this pattern is repeated world-wide. Some women in Standing's sample do control at least some of their finance in the narrow sense but the context has social and cultural underpinnings which in the main militate against women's autonomy. What of a mother who has her own bank account in order to save up for the daughter's dowry? Is she being autonomous or simply encouraging 'a further entrenchment of gender hierarchies?' (Standing, 1975).

There are other problems. As Afshar (1985) points out: '... where women are physically separated from access to the cash economy and need to rely on men as intermediaries, their ability to engage in petty commodity production may in fact exacerbate their subordination'. Women who cannot sell their labour directly are often commercially exploited by the middlemen who are in a position to profit from

**Who keeps her own income?**

**TABLE V – Control of income by age and workplace**

**Meena Bazaar**

| AGE | YES | NO | SOME | DON'T KNOW |
|---|---|---|---|---|
| Under 20 | 1 | 2 | 1 | 0 |
| 20-30 | 4 | 2 | 0 | 0 |
| 30-40 | 1 | 0 | 0 | 0 |
| 40+ | 4 | 0 | 0 | 0 |
| TOTAL | 10 | 4 | 1 | 0 |

**Retail**

| AGE | YES | NO | SOME | DON'T KNOW |
|---|---|---|---|---|
| Under 20 | 0 | 0 | 0 | 0 |
| 20-30 | 1 | 0 | 0 | 3 |
| 30-40 | 0 | 0 | 0 | 0 |
| 40+ | 0 | 2 | 1 | 0 |
| TOTAL | 1 | 2 | 1 | 3 |

**Teachers**

| AGE | YES | NO | SOME | DON'T KNOW |
|---|---|---|---|---|
| Under 20 | 0 | 0 | 0 | 0 |
| 20-30 | 3 | 1 | 0 | 1 |
| 30-40 | 4 | 1 | 1 | 0 |
| 40+ | 3 | 0 | 0 | 0 |
| TOTAL | 10 | 2 | 1 | 1 |

**Manufacturing**

| AGE | YES | NO | SOME | DON'T KNOW |
|---|---|---|---|---|
| Under 20 | 0 | 0 | 0 | 0 |
| 20-30 | 1 | 2 | 0 | 0 |
| 30-40 | 4 | 1 | 0 | 0 |
| 40+ | 4 | 1 | 0 | 0 |
| TOTAL | 9 | 4 | 0 | 0 |

**Total**

| AGE | YES | NO | SOME | DON'T KNOW | TOTAL |
|---|---|---|---|---|---|
| Under 20 | 1 | 2 | 1 | 0 | 4 |
| 20-30 | 9 | 5 | 0 | 4 | 18 |
| 30-40 | 9 | 2 | 1 | 2 | 14 |
| 40+ | 11 | 3 | 1 | 0 | 15 |
| TOTAL | 30 | 12 | 3 | 6 | 51 |

**Table VI: Percentage of age group keeping income (excluding don't know category)**

| AGE | % |
|---|---|
| Under 20 | 25% |
| 20-30 | 63% |
| 30-40 | 69% |
| 40+ | 78% |

women's work. Meena Bazaar, as a women-only workplace with a female clientele, is one example of how this problem can be overcome.

More conventionally, 'The production of sons in these situations is the only solution to lightening the burden of work as well as contributing to status they wouldn't otherwise have' (Afshar, 1985). In the Meena Bazaar many of the women of child-bearing age were not married. In teaching, also, many women were unmarried and were reliant not upon middlemen but on the educational establishment hierarchy, which contained many women. However, it is difficult to make generalisations from these two situations as they are in many ways atypical work situations for women.

There is also a wide range of systems of financial management within the families of the women interviewed. These range from women keeping their own income and controlling their husbands' earnings, to handing their income to another member of the family. There appears to be little difference in the numbers of women who keep their own income in the different employment categories. Although the samples were very small, they show little differences along class lines.

Many working-class women in the sample had no husband, whether through death or divorce, and so were the 'head of the household' in the Western sense and there-fore not typical. However, this 'head of household' definition may be misleading because the husband's relatives would normally assume the responsibility for the household after his death. A women's control of financial matters is therefore not synonymous with the absence of a male partner.

Ten out of fourteen teachers kept their income, one kept some and gave the rest to her mother. One gave hers to her mother-in-law; one bore the financial respon-sibility for the whole family without spelling out how, and one did not say. Two of the women who kept their income were not married. One kept her husband's income as well, and another said that her husband did not even know how much she earned. Two of them said they kept control but gave some money to the family.

Women interviewed were not asked specifically about their spending habits but those in the manufacturing sector were found to be more likely than others to use their money on basic necessities. This may be because they were more likely to be working out of economic necessity. In Islamic tradition, the responsibility of looking after wife and children rests with the husband. The wife has no obligation to contribute to the family budget, and she can keep her own income whether inherited or earned. This tradition of not having to rely on the income of women to support the family now transcends religious boundaries. This may go some way to explain why girls and women from better-off homes can keep their income and take it with them when they get married or spend it on 'non-essentials' like education. One teacher, for example, kept both her income and that of her husband, but her earnings went to the education of children, whilst her husband's went towards the basic necessities of the home. However, the tradition of women's income not being put towards the family budget does not always apply across the social spectrum; it is partly dependent on the economic position of the family.

## Aspirations, education and outcome

The women interviewed dispelled many stereotypes. Virtually all wanted to work; some had to struggle for the right. Family expectations varied, and some families were open to persuasion on the question of undertaking paid work. Many women had high aspirations and several were encouraged by their families. Many had difficulty reconciling domestic responsibilities with employment opportunities, but this was not because of their religious background, as the analysis of purdah illustrates. The evidence throughout shows that these problems transcend social and national boundaries.

Educational and employment aspirations are not necessarily the same; an interplay of complex factors determines their fulfillment: parental wishes, the financial position of the family and practical support. Whether the women chose to give their career a high priority over other areas of their lives, such as the needs of their husbands, was also important, as was the existence of a women-only workplace.

The women made decisions about the family budget, the education of their children, their own education and their careers. Many worked to improve the employment opportunities for women in general, especially those who were in influential positions and could act as role models. Many of them were clear about the constraints upon them as women and sought to challenge them. Some did so by pursuing higher education, others by undertaking careers which were traditionally considered as the male preserve. Yet others attempted to ensure that their daughters would have better life chances through education. These decisions were considered and active, not in keeping with the stereotype of Asian women in Britain and much of the West as passive victims. Nor does the stereotype that 'Asian women have no financial control' hold up. Nearly sixty per cent of the women interviewed kept all their earned income. Many had a great deal of financial control. There is a complex interaction of factors which determines whether women earn an income, keep their earnings and have control over how they are spent.

As we saw in the section on purdah, both Muslim and Hindu women have often striven against the constraints imposed on them, and have achieved higher status because of that. They fought against male domination in the pre- and post-colonial periods, against colonial role and the new form of imported patriarchy that was brought with it. The interviews showed that women still seek to improve their situation. Whilst there may be commonality of experience among women across the world, socio-economic and political systems create distinct differences. Asian women in Britain have had to contend with the extra dimension of racism. The interviews have shown a great diversity of experience between the women; in refuting one set of stereotypes it is important to guard against substituting another.

Employment was seen by many women in broader terms than career aspirations; they recognised how they could affect the lives of other women by opening up employment opportunities and other facilities, such as banking by women for women. Informal networks always existed but are now being supplemented by formal structures. The support of women for others has happened in all workplaces and cuts across religious and political boundaries.

The interviews showed that control of finance was complex. Economic necessity within the family seemed to be the most important determinant of how earnings were spent. The ability to earn and the control of income were not synonymous; some women handed their earnings to others in the family whereas others controlled income which they themselves did not earn. Status within the family and society does not depend necessarily on earning capacity; it is related also to gender, age and social class.

All those interviewed were ordinary women leading normal lives. They were acutely aware of the complexity of the society in which they lived and the particular constraints it put on them. Shaheed and Mumtaz (1987) observe:

> It is impossible to describe that composite of various averages, the Pakistani woman, for the simple reason that like all other stereotypes, which pass for reality, she does not exist. In Pakistan, as in other Third World countries, it is perhaps even more difficult to identify the average woman than in the industrialised countries because the uneven penetration of firstly colonial rule, and subsequently, capitalist modes of production, have meant that a Pakistani woman's life can have remained petrified for centuries, or have been radically altered by the cataclysmic events of her people's history.

Whilst it may be difficult to draw broad conclusions from the evidence of these interviews, they clearly demonstrate the diversity of familial and financial arrangements, even within the same social class. They also illustrate the commonality of women's class position across national and international boundaries. For example, women from economical and emotionally secure backgrounds are more likely to realise their ambitions for professional careers than those who are less privileged. In this respect, migration to affluent conditions, such as North America offers to many, can be advantageous to Asian women – provided that they and their families are not oppressed because of their ethnic origins.

Chapter 5

# The Asian Family

Chains of blood gripping tight
Marriage contracts slipping by
Waves of love spring and die.
In the family bosom I laugh and cry
at the loss and gain of bonding ties

The family is the central pivot of our society. How its values and functions shape the socio-psychological realities of the individual has exercised the minds of politicians, theologians, statisticians sociologists, social anthropologists and educationalists. Statisticians map out the number of family break-ups and economists calculate its cost to society. Sociologists define for us the nuclear and extended family arrangements and anthropologists take us on a journey to polygynous and polyandrous settings. An array of voices from the right, left and centre political parties speak in a chorus on defending family values. The chorus reaches a crescendo when joined by religious leaders and even pop stars.

The mass media constantly remind us of the unacceptably high break-up of families in the West. The highest of all is in the US where nearly a third of all new marriages end in divorce, followed by England and Wales. (*Guardian,* 17 June, and 13 August 1996).

The family not only dominates the socio-political and moral agendas but also haunts the individual's socio-psychic world. Individuals seem almost to spend their entire lives either fulfilling or pushing against the parameters set by the family. Are features and values uniform in a given society, or are they class- or even region-specific? Are all families in one socio-economic and cultural setting the same or are they subject to individual variation?

As religious and political leaders across the world claim the family as one of the central tenents of their belief systems, its break-up is perceived as a threat to the very fabric of society of which it is a central point. Founding fathers of world religions and political ideologies had an ambivalent attitude to and relationship with their families. The Buddha left his family and the princely state in search of enlightenment. The prophet Muhammad moved away from his only close relative, his uncle, to form his new religion: Islam. Guru Nanak and Jesus never married. Karl Marx's marriage was less than ideal. They all subordinated allegiance to the family to allegiance to ideology or philosophical principles.

The colonial legacy, the subsequent partition of the Subcontinent, the Second World War and immigration to the West have all profoundly affected the Asian family. Yet it is still viewed as a monolithic creature with its tentacles deeply embedded in the soil of the Subcontinent, solid and unchanging. This notion nurtures a set of stereotypes, stereotypes that are dangerous because they are largely untrue and also because they underlie many key decisions about health, education and community policies. (These are examined in detail in the following chapters.)

The principal stereotypes about Asian families can be caricatured as follows, with only a little exaggeration:

**Ghetto mentality** They stay in their own little ghetto. There is no escape from the all-pervading family. They don't want to mix, they keep their women hidden away under voluminous robes and head coverings.

**Large extended families** The families are very large, with married children and grandparents all living together packed into restricted accommodation.

**Arranged marriages with close relatives** They have arranged marriages. They tend to marry their cousins or other very close family members.

**Limited horizons and ambitions for women** The women are tied to the kitchen sink and can't think further than feeding their men and looking after the children. Their horizons are very limited. In public, they walk three paces behind their husbands.

**Many children** They have lots of children – 'they breed like rabbits' – the women are nothing but reproductive machines.

**The children's cognitive development is retarded by their home environment** This stereotype is attributed to three main factors:

–   They don't speak English at home. They don't watch the same television programmes or read the same newspapers as everybody else; all they watch is frivolous Indian film videos. If they don't know English they can't think properly.

–   They spend all their time indoors, and hardly ever go out.

–   They don't have toys to play with.

## The reality behind the stereotypes

### Ghetto mentality

This, like the other stereotypes, is based on the assumption that the Asians are a homogeneous group with no class, religio-cultural or geographical differences. But closer scrutiny presents a different and much more complex picture.

Like all social groups, some people want to live in close proximity with those who share a common lifestyle and ways of thinking, while others are more individualistic and want a more diverse experience. For example, there are two opposed viewpoints current in the Asian community about who should be responsible for the delivery of their social services: one group holds that Asians should be catered for by Asians, who understand them better, while the other maintains that it is preferable to deal with a complete stranger who will not 'leak' private information within the Asian community. A similar dichotomy of opinion exists where children's education is concerned.

Asians who made the journey to Britain came via such diverse routes as the West Indies, Indian Ocean islands, and latterly East Africa, as well as the Subcontinent itself. Often the only common denominator amongst these groups is that their ancestors originated from the Subcontinent. In many other significant ways they are very different. For example, many Asians from the Caribbean islands speak only English and wear Western clothes, and some who were originally Hindu or Muslim have converted to Christianity, or have made marriages which cross religious and/or racial lines and adopt a pragmatic attitude to religion. Asians from Mauritius may speak English and French in addition to their heritage language and wear Western clothes. East Africans may speak one or more of the Subcontinent languages of their ancestors with an African influence. For instance, East African Asians even when speaking Panjabi or Gujerati may refer to broom and mop as *fugia* and *fungusa* respectively. This is no different from the British during the Raj adopting local words such as *tiffin* for lunch. There are vast differences between urban and rural dwellers from the Subcontinent. Two Oxbridge graduates, one Asian and one English, have more in common than two people of the same ethnic group but from a different class.

So-called Asians, as different from one another as from the white majority, have been thrown together by force of circumstances. Most lived together in cheaper housing areas because it was possible initially to rent and later purchase property more easily from other Asian people than from white people. This arrangement was tolerated because most people saw it as a temporary phenomenon – men, who had generally emigrated first, leaving their families behind, intended to stay for only a short time before returning to their home countries. This became increasingly impractical and their families gradually began to join them. The housing situation continued to exhibit the same pattern: poorer areas of urban decay were occupied by Asians. Added to the general decline in housing was 'white flight': as the numbers of Asians in an area increased, the original inhabitants fled to other often more prosperous parts of cities, taking with them, it seems, the previous amenities, particularly street cleaning and rubbish collection. Just as in housing, so in education: as soon as the number of non-white families exceeded the magical figure of ten to twenty per cent the general decline set in. As Asians became more established and wanted to move to outer suburban areas, they were confronted with two problems: proprietors who did not want to sell their houses to Asians, and mortgage lending institutions operating what came to be known as the 'red lining' policy. An investigation in Rochdale by the Commission for Racial Equality (CRE) revealed that mortgage lenders operated an informal policy of not granting loans to black people on houses in areas deemed too good for them to inhabit (CRE, 1985). The problem of housing was by no means confined to owner occupier or private rented accommodation: it extended to borough and city council practice. These democratically elected councils also operated discriminatory polices so Asian families often could not secure council rented property and the housing allocated was more likely to be in run-down areas where families were frequently subjected to racial harassment. The London boroughs of Hackney and Tower Hamlets were equally inhospitable.

Although British institutions operate a blanket policy towards Asians, differences between them remain. Some Asians, by virtue of their religion (Christianity), education or family background (for example their service in the armed forces), may identify more with white British than Asian culture; some may choose a hybrid or extremely multicultural, cosmopolitan or Bohemian existence; yet in the context of Britain they are all lumped together as 'Asians'. Conversely, the children of very Westernised or liberal parents who are born and brought up in Britain may choose to reject their parents' value systems and adopt a stricter code of dress or belief systems. Cultural or religious purists may perceive their families as deviating too far from the true religion or customs, being too heavily affected by outside influences. For orthodox Hindus and Sikhs, these 'outside influences' could be cohabitation with Islam in the Subcontinent over hundreds of years, and vice versa. For Parsis, it could be the effect of Buddhism. For all of them it might be the British colonial presence in the Subcontinent and the alien culture in contemporary Britain or North America. Individuals might cross religio-cultural boundaries by adopting a religion or life style different from their families'. In some cases they may reject or be rejected by their families.

Whilst it may be true that many Asians live in fairly closed communities in Britain, this is far from universal. One may cite many cases of Asian families who moved to the suburbs in the early seventies, against all the odds, in order to live in a mixed community and send their children to schools with the white majority.

## Large extended families

Asian families are just as varied as their Western counterparts. Family patterns, determined both by economics and by choice, are very diverse. Asian families in Britain and the Subcontinent range from two or three generations living in one homestead headed by the eldest male or female, through nuclear families to single-parent families and people living alone in their own homes.

None of the families I stayed with in the Subcontinent had more than three or four children; two couples had none. Of all those I stayed with, only one in Bombay and one in Hyderabad followed the same faith for three generations, Hindu in one case and Parsi in the other. The family in Hyderabad had unmarried twin daughters in their thirties who followed professional careers and had no plans to marry. Another Muslim family in Hyderabad was made up of three sons headed by a single father. His wife had left him for being too modern by bringing her out of purdah – she felt it was not appropriate for a woman of her aristocratic background. Two of the women I met lived on their own: one a school inspector in Karachi, and another a Christian divorcee in Bangalore. Two of the women I interviewed in Calderdale had no children; one lived on her own two hundred miles away from her family.

Couples may live separately or with their in-laws. In some communities it is customary for the bride to follow her husband, usually to his familial home. This is known as going to *susral*. In others the groom comes to live with the bride in her natal home – *ghur damad*. Irrespective of the physical arrangements, the members of each family may be close or distant. For example a single woman living on her own in the south of England may be very close to her family who live two or three hundred miles away and take all important decisions in consultation. A married man living with his parents, on the other hand, may choose to have only a super-ficial relationship with his natal family. In certain cases emotional ties with in-laws or 'adopted ' relatives may be stronger than with 'real' ones. There are a number of ways in which an individual can be incorporated into the family: being breast-fed by the same woman, eating out of the same plate, sharing the dinner table or even sitting on the same seat. This may even occur between members of the opposite sex, for whom that degree of proximity would normally be considered unusual.

'Adopted' relatives perform rights and duties which would be indistinguishable from those demanded of blood ties. The Hindu/Sikh tradition of *rukshabundan* in which a sister ties a ceremonial strands of thread around a brother's wrist is a for-mal acceptance of the general principle. The brother in question could be a blood relative, a stranger or indeed her brother. This custom of bringing strangers into the familial relationship can be invoked to guard against the possibility of sexual harassment, or to include people across the religious divide. Hindu men, for example, would 'adopt' Muslim or Sikh women as their sisters and vice versa. An older man could 'adopt' a daughter, son, niece or nephew simply by placing his hand on the individual's head and referring to them in terms of the desired or intended relationship. A woman can do likewise. On occasions, members of the in-laws' family are 'adopted' in as part of the natal system. For instance, if there is a long-standing friendship between two people of same sex and one of them later contracts a marriage with the other's sibling, the former relationship may continue to receive precedence over the latter. Indeed on important matters the technical 'sister-in-law' may choose to act as if she were the bride's sister. This arrangement can be replicated across other relationships.

The system of accepting outsiders into the family highlights the society's flexibility in its general trend of segregating the sexes. It also enables close bonds between people of the opposite sex across the religious or social divide. These ties of kinship can be passed down the generations, as indeed can feuds. This is one example of how the rules of purdah are applied in practice. English novelist E M Forster provides an insight into this custom in *A Passage To India* (1936), when Dr. Aziz offers a most precious gift by showing the photograph of his deceased wife to his friend Fielding. The two characters are from different racial and religious backgrounds and they represent the colonised and the coloniser. The event is particularly significant because it happens at a time when political tension between the two communities is especially high. When Fielding raises the question of purdah, which would have prohibited him from ever seeing Dr. Aziz's wife, Dr. Aziz replies that she would have overcome the barrier by calling him brother. This depiction of the bond between the two friends, which is then extended to the woman, in this case Dr. Aziz's deceased wife is an illustration of how the institution of purdah and the family operate in practice.

'Adopted' or other relatives can take on crucial functions in the lives of individuals in general and women in particular. An 'adopted' uncle, mother or sister may, in certain circumstances, take the responsibility and privileges for the entire or partial welfare of the whole family or particular individuals in it – from educating them to arranging their marriage. When marriages are arranged, various members, especially those responsible for it, keep a watchful eye on the young couple to ensure that any sign of physical or emotional problems are dealt with at the earliest opportunity. This is in recognition of the fact that there needs to be a period of adjustment to the new relationship, even if the marriage is between relatives. Couples are seldom left to sort out their own problems: indeed they are often tutored in the art of courtship during the early period of their marriage. The bride can be pampered for several weeks, during which she wears a new outfit every day from the dowry provided by natal and marital families. She is the centre of attention, exempt from household chores and cooking. Her 'coming out' is traditionally marked by a ceremony in which she prepares a sweet dish for guests invited for the occasion. This custom appears to be common, with individual variations across the religious divide in the north of the Subcontinent. Its practice even in the West is evident although less elaborate. It is not always possible for a busy bride, who may have taken a couple of weeks off from her studies or work, to allow herself the luxury of being the *dulhan*. A contributory factor to the increased divorce rate amongst Asians in Britain may be that couples no longer have enough time to iron out potential areas of difficulty while supported by others.

## Arranged marriages with close relatives

In some villages in the Subcontinent, the entire community can be related through blood and marital relationships. In the case of Muslims, Parsi and Hindus from southern India both are possible. The Parsi communities are concentrated in urban areas and, being a minority, do not occupy whole villages. For northern Hindus and Sikhs marriages within the same villages are often avoided, sometimes even taboo, as people from the same village are considered a part of the kinship with whom marriage is disallowed. But among Hindus in southern India in Karnataka and Andhra Pradesh, for example, a woman can marry her maternal uncle or his children, but not her maternal aunt's children. After marriage to her uncle a woman may go and live with him in his house, or they may set up a separate homestead. Similarly a man can marry his father's sister or her children, but a woman cannot marry her paternal uncle or his children. Muslims can marry first cousins on either side but not maternal or paternal uncles or aunts.

Just as the eligibility of a marriage partner varies between different religious or regional groupings, so do attitudes to marriage. For Christians, marriage is supposed to be made in heaven and the contract is witnessed by God to be broken only by death. For Hindus it goes even further: it is a sacrament not severed at death, hence the justification for sati. Marriage for Muslims, however, is a social contract, the detail of which can be written in. Marriages may be arranged or otherwise contracted: they can be with blood relatives, for example cousins whom they have known since childhood, or with strangers. One of my hosts in Mysore, a Hindu Brahmin, was married to her maternal uncle, with whom she lived, and referred to him as *mama* (maternal uncle). The two sons, who were unmarried, lived and worked elsewhere in India, but she was intending to arrange their marriages. On the other hand her niece, with whom I stayed in Bengalore, married someone she had met whilst at university in Delhi and had no children. My host in Bombay, a Parsi, lived with her husband, mother and one daughter. She and her husband lived in her mother's home. One of her sisters was married to a Muslim, and whilst she still regarded herself as a Parsi, her children were brought up as Muslims. Both of my own cousins in Karachi chose their own partners: neither was from the same ethnic or socio-economic grouping. In addition, the younger's wife is from the Shiite sect of Islam whilst he is from the Sunni – potentially at least as problematic as marriage between Catholics and Protestants in Northern Ireland. Neither is particularly strong in their religious conviction and it was obviously not an issue for them.

Mixed marriages are far from unknown between Parsi, Muslim, Hindu, Sikh, Jew, Christian or Buddhist. Attitudes towards marriage may be determined by not only religious or ethnic grouping but also the general ambience surrounding them. General social circumstance is important in shaping people's attitudes. Some may take on the values of the majority culture of the country; others may react against it and adopt a more fundamental or purist attitude to their heritage.

## Limited horizons and ambitions for women

There is very little truth in this stereotype, as my research in the Subcontinent and Britain shows. Parents of many women in both samples went to extraordinary lengths to ensure a brighter future for their daughters. Particularly noteworthy is the number of parents in Halifax who had arranged private tuition for their children – including daughters – because they wanted them to succeed educationally and professionally, often despite being themselves unemployed. Some encouraged their children to apply to the local grant maintained schools, formerly grammar schools, and succeeded in securing places.

There are, of course, other ambitions, not least those that women may have within their own family, whatever their background or earning power. Even the most superficial acquaintance with Asian families reveals an intricate web of power relations. Families may be patrilineal and patriarchal, but the eldest woman in the family seems to wield enormous power. She invariably decides on the menu for the family, so controlling the food budget and the kinds of food consumed.

The responsibility for family finances including the welfare of the wife rests with the husband, as head of the household. Some men may have control over the outside world but be intimidated by the women in the home and the eldest woman in particular, especially as important decisions about who marries whom are invariably made by the women or with their genuine agreement. Without the active co-operation of women the whole system of arranged marriages would probably collapse. Women are centre stage, from making dowries and wedding arrangements to actually asking for the hand in marriage of a partner for their son, daughter or other relative. In Muslim families it is customary for the female's family to be approached; for northern Hindus the reverse is the case. Older women's opinions in domestic matters almost automatically carry more weight than those of younger men and women, even when the latter have the benefit of formal education and earning power.

The number of shops run and owned by Asian women in certain areas of Britain is noteworthy. A sizeable proportion of Asian shops selling groceries, dress fabrics and ready-made clothes in the Hyde Park area of Leeds, the White Abbey Road area of Bradford and the Belgrave area of Leicester are run by women. Their presence is also felt on the Leeds market. Women in this occupation vary in age, religious backgrounds and mode of dress. Some wear *shalwar qumeez* and have the *duputta* over their heads; others wear the former but no head covering; others wear saris, dresses or jeans. What is clear is that these Asian women have business acumen and are making a financial contribution to their own lives and to society at large, often without any formal training in business or any financial help from the banks.

The difficulties encountered by the community over securing business loans from mainstream financial institutions is outside the remit of the present study. However, women in the Subcontinent have a historic 'banking collective' known as *beesi* or *cammity*. This tradition has been transported to the diaspora and is used to finance a host of commitments from weddings to businesses. A group of individuals agree to contribute a fixed sum of money on a weekly or a monthly basis for a specified time. Each person draws an equal share during the life of the venture. This way of gaining control over their financial lives has proved invaluable in the history of women's co-operatives in the Subcontinent, which include fishing and fabric printing. The idea underlies the setting up of the women-only bank in Bangalore described in Chapter 4.

## Many children

Not all Asians have large numbers of children and some have no children by design. The number of children is subject to social trends and economic needs of a society at a given point in its history. Asians in the West, like other immigrant communities who move into a different culture, have tended to adopt the ways of the dominant culture within a generation or two. However, like many Catholics, some orthodox Muslims or Hindus regard children as a gift from God. Others may choose a more flexible approach and be guided by their ability to provide materially for their children. In some middle-class families in which women pursue demanding professional careers, the lack of adequate child care facilities could prove the determining factor. Like their white counterparts, middle-class Asians are more likely to have fewer children than working-class Asians.

## Children's cognitive development is retarded

It is true that many Asian families do not use much English at home, and this should be no surprise. It is not natural for people to speak to their closest relatives in a language with which they have little or no emotional involvement. For many Asians English is, at best, an adopted language, a *lingua franca* used for commercial or official purposes. It is no different from the English speaking English in the home when they emigrate to France, Spain or anywhere else – and *they* often go one step further and send their children to English-medium schools.

Many educationalists in Britain argue that one of the main causes for Asian children's educational underachievement is their lack of fluency in English, because English is not used in the home. Even the Swann Report (1985) regards the English language as the unifying factor for all British citizens. This mode of thinking is unhelpful in a pluralist society in which communities take pride in maintaining their heritage languages.

Further, if educational achievement were dependent solely or even significantly on the use of English in the home then all English-speaking pupils would succeed equally in the world of academe and the Welsh would do worse than native English-speaking children. (Research shows that the British educational system is much more class-biased than language-biased, militating against the working-classes.) But the Cox Report tested Welsh and English children at the age of 11, and found that there was no difference in their linguistic competence. Similarly, many Asians achieve academic excellence despite English not being their home language. A significant number of eminent writers in English – Tagore and Idris Shah among them – are not native speakers of English.

There is no evidence that Asians watch more or less English television than the population at large. It would be of interest to conduct a survey to elicit information on the television habits of Asians and also whether the general run of non-Asian videos are more informative than Indian films.

As far as 'going out' is concerned, cultures which have emerged from a hotter climate are more likely to spend their time outdoors than those in colder climates. A cursory observation of the difference in architecture bears witness to this. English homes are closed, whereas traditional homes in the Subcontinent often have inner courtyards open to the sky and modern urban flats have balconies. Nonetheless, children in Asian families, unlike those in the majority British culture, are an integral part of a social experience. Unless they are asleep, they participate in the adult world, which in turn is profoundly affected by them.

White educators seem to believe that going to the theatre or museums, for instance, constitutes 'going out' but that visiting relatives is tantamount to 'staying in'. This also applies to visiting the Subcontinent or the country of their families' origin. It is ironic that a visit to the gallery of Primitive and Oriental Arts in Knaresborough in Yorkshire, which displays exhibits from 'other cultures', is classed as educational, whereas staying with relatives in the Subcontinent who may be using similar objects in context is considered as detracting from the educational process. School exchanges to Europe or America are organised to provide a balanced experience and broaden children's horizons, yet Asian children's visits to the Subcontinent, which call for a far greater degree of cultural and emotional adjustment, are often ignored or deplored.

Asian families may or may not buy less toys, but this misses the point. The question for mainstream educational thought is: why is contact with toys considered superior to encountering real-life situations? In Asian families it is scarcely assumed that toys are a substitute for human contact.

As has been illustrated throughout this chapter it is difficult to arrive at a common definition of the family, and this is true for its values and functions. The huge historic and geographic variations have contributed to the racial, cultural, linguistic and religious mix of that society and these are reflected in family relationships and also class and caste divisions.

The values of a family may be either influenced or determined by a host of different factors including religion, class and economic position. Individuals within Asian families do challenge the extolling of so-called family values when they conflict with their own sense of right or wrong, whether over appropriate clothing or political or religious beliefs. The family can be a fulfilling and enriching experience for all concerned; it can also be the source of unhappiness and suffering. The family is the unit in which most individuals spend their formative years and it shapes their later personalities. This experience could be inherently negative or positive, but the individual's interpretation of events and her adult recollections may not reflect that reality.

## The consequences of stereotyping

The Calderdale study is one illustration of the mismatch of perception between the ambitions of Asian women themselves, their parents and white professionals. The experience of many in the sample, supported by other research (Eggleston, 1986; Swann, 1985; Leeds City Council, 1997) is that teachers and other educational professionals still hold negative stereotypes of Asian females, and this affects their performance. Careers advice is based more on stereotypes of the 'Asian family' than on the individual. Educators may be concerned that girls will marry early but marriage does not necessarily constitute an end to a girl's education or career. Several women I interviewed had young children who were being cared for by their mothers or mothers-in-law whilst they pursued their careers. Asian families are thus as complex and varied as any Western family and sweeping generalisations which affect the individual's life chances are without foundation.

Chapter 6

# Asian Women in a Town in Northern England

Alien soil rejects our roots
Efforts made to preserve the shoots.

This chapter draws on a case study of Asian women in an English town. Experience of living in the West is contrasted with the lives and opportunities of women in the Subcontinent. It begins with a general overview of the national and international events which have shaped women's history in Britain and addresses the mythological notion of a static utopian ideal. Throughout history women's position is affected by economic and political changes which in turn influence social trends. The impact of two World Wars has been felt profoundly by women across the globe.

## The colonial context

The two World Wars destroyed the old world order. The Ottoman and the Hapsburg empires collapsed and sowed the seeds for the contraction and final fall of the European empires. In 1947 in India, the sun began to set on the British empire, and Britain's focus of attention shifted from a global policy of maintaining the empire to rebuilding the home country after the destruction suffered by the World Wars, especially the second. Peoples from the former colonies who had been called upon for help in the war effort were once again asked for help. They were given work vouchers and granted permanent right of abode in Britain with full citizenship, rights which were later eroded.

The communal tensions in the Subcontinent which had been fuelled by the efforts of the British colonial power to create divisions between the religious communities culminated in bloody partition along religious lines of India and Pakistan as two separate states. In the ensuing confusion Sikhs, Muslims and Hindus were killed.

Whole communities that had lived in relative harmony for over a thousand years were ripped apart. Millions were displaced, fleeing their ancestral lands to save their lives. This ready-made army of the dispossessed was conveniently recruited as labour for the post-war economic boom in Britain. Most of these immigrants were actively recruited and the ex-servicemen who wished to stay behind after the second World War were allowed to do so. When Enoch Powell was Secretary of State for Health in the 1960s, he recruited health service workers in the West Indies and this continued right up until 1984. Similar drives for immigration into Britain were conducted in the Indian Subcontinent and other former colonies. Some immigrants came as a result of the break-up of empire; the Indians in East Africa – originally brought there as indentured labour – were issued with British passports at the point of independence of the countries in question. When, some years later, the ruling African élite began to bring in more stringent rules and regulations against the export of capital and started the process of withdrawing of the privileges which the Indians had enjoyed under British rule, large numbers of East African Asians sought to exercise their right of abode in Britain. This led to increasing resistance from the British government, which by a unique act in 1968 denied British Asians from Kenya who held British passports the rights of entry into Britain. This resistence reached its crescendo in 1972 when Idi Amin expelled the Asian community *en masse* from Uganda.

Little real preparation, in the form of psychological or social adjustment, or even adequate housing, was made for these immigrants. The education of their children, in particular teaching them English, became an overwhelming issue for some local education authorities (LEAs), which established language centres for those immigrant children. Through Section 11 of the 1966 Local Government Act, a fund was set up for the children from the New Commonwealth to learn English. At about the same time, immigration controls were set to restrict the numbers of settlers from the New Commonwealth, itself a euphemism to separate white from black. This trend has continued; the politics of 'racial equality' in Britain became inextricably intertwined with immigration controls. The raising of the bogey of mass immigration became a favourite ploy of the government or of politicians seeking easy popularity. Roy Hattersley, MP for Sparkbrook in Birmingham, was sharply critical. He said: 'The disgrace of immigration policy, as presently operated, is not that too many people are coming into this country. The shame is that men and women who should be allowed to enter Britain are being kept out' (*Guardian*, May, 1994).

One continued side-effect of these intertwined policies has been the identification of even the grandchildren of primary immigrants as 'immigrants' and never, somehow, as British; another has been to hamper and frustrate the process of reuniting families where 'immigrants' are involved. Another effect of history has been to demonise Muslims, who are seen as particularly alien and dangerous. They are characterised by such phrases as 'fundamentalist' and, especially since the Gulf War, portrayed as fanatical and warloving – and certainly not as good British citizens. The disproportionate contribution of many Muslim soldiers to the British war effort far from their own homes and interests is generally forgotten, along with the contributions of Sikhs and Hindus. They are – unjustifiably – portrayed as a burden on the country's resources.

Case law in the West shows that the judiciary is ill-informed about laws such as India's Dowry Prohibition Act, 1961. This means that Asian women in the diaspora are unlikely to secure justice in dowry disputes and related violence. The case of Tasleem Sadiq, murdered in 1995 because her in-laws were shamed by the 'sin' of her affair was another instance of injustice: the establishment, judicial and social, blamed her background but showed little understanding of it. All over the world, and in most histories, women who transgress against the accepted sexual code are treated more harshly than men. When Queen Dido of Carthage is abandoned by her lover Aeneas, she has no option but to commit suicide, out of grief, while he sails away to found Rome.

Whenever the situation of women undergoes change, as with the recent ordination of women as priests in the Church of England, every effort is made to allow for the sensibilities of men resistant to that change. Men seek always to enlist the help of God, society, the family and the state to define and confine the roles of women.

And how do women cope with this external control of their actions and behaviour? Some fight; there are many historical and modern casualties. Some survive by internalising these external constraints, accepting the role defined for them and submitting even to the extremes of sati or infibulation. As women lack power in their own right they become the custodians of a cultural norm which often militates against the liberation of their sex.

When women do not conform, the law is severe. Wife-battering has, until recently, been largely ignored by the forces of law and order, reluctant to intrude upon 'domestic' violence. This attitude has begun to change, in part due to the pressure from women's organisations. Yet when a man goes so far as to kill his wife, the law is often lenient about attacks 'committed in the heat of the moment'. Pleas of mitigating circumstances have included references to the wife's nagging behaviour. But if a wife is driven by ill-treatment to kill her husband, she may be given a harsh sentence because her act is deemed to have been premeditated. Kiranjit Ahluwalia served four years in jail for killing her abusive husband while he slept; it required sustained lobbying by women's organisations for the law to be changed to recognise her plight. The double standards of sexual mores can be supported by the grim-faced wives of politicians who 'forgive' their husbands for sexual transgressions which are widely publicised in the media.

Western society's view of Asian women is largely uncomprehending; they are seen as quiescent, uncomplaining, passive and put-upon. Their subjection to infinite indignities is assumed; their resistance and resilience always surprises. Yet even within their traditional cultural confines, women have considerable freedom of self-expression; historical commentators have noticed the freedom existing behind the veil. When a practice was unacceptable, women rebelled. Much of the investigation into the 'sati' of Roop Kanwar in India was led by campaigning women's organisations. In the Israeli village of Dir Hanna a 23-year old Arab woman, Ataf el-Habib, recently led 120 local women in a successful three-year struggle against the Tel Aviv industrialists who paid them less than the national minimum wage for their work. Women also champion the cause of other disadvantaged groups. Most women's organisations have campaigned for more vigorous defence of abused children and this includes Asian women's organisations, confronting instances of such abuse within their own communities.

The position of Asian women in Britain is a function not only of their position as members of an immigrant community, but also of their gender. So they also share the problems of British women in general, and it is this issue to which I now turn.

## Women at work in England since 1800

Both the role of women and the way in which work is organised have changed greatly over the past two hundred years, and most significantly in the last twenty. Before the Industrial Revolution, most women in the West worked as part of a team involving husband, children and other relatives, in occupations which allowed them to combine child-care and housework with earning money. They spun the thread which their men wove into cloth; they weeded fields and cleared stones, made clothes, brewed beer, hawked the fish their husbands caught or even accompanied them down the mines as tub hauliers. The needs of industry to concentrate workers on industrial premises forced women into factories and to neglect their domestic roles. By 1851 one third of all women worked outside the home, in the textile industries of Lancashire and Yorkshire, in the Black Country factories, or in domestic service. Almost everywhere they worked, their wages were lower than those of men, and their labour was often dispensed with as soon as they married. When married women attempted to combine child-care with paid work, they either had to do extremely ill-paid work at home, or attempt somehow to juggle the two. Women were excluded from the better-paid and more highly-skilled occupations. Elizabeth Garrett, who struggled to qualify as a doctor in Britain in 1870, did not know that Doctor 'James' Barrie, with whom Florence Nightingale quarrelled bitterly in the Crimean War, had become an extremely successful doctor some years earlier by passing herself off as a man.

Women finally achieved some economic control over their lives once the Married Women's Property Act of 1870 finally abolished the rule which had put all women's wealth under their husbands' control. This enabled an unhappily-married woman of family means to live separately from her husband without descending into complete poverty. The First World War marked a watershed; women took part in many areas from which they had previously been excluded and made decisions in their lives, including radically changing their mode of dress, styles of hair and their sexual behaviour. Skirts which had swept to the ankle were shortened, for practical reasons.

At the end of the war, when the men came home, skirts became shorter still and even more women bobbed their hair – despite the banishment of women from many of the workplaces they had so recently entered. However, women remained in offices as typists and telephonists, because they had proved themselves both useful and cheap. The first extension of suffrage to women was achieved in 1918, although only in selected categories. With women moving once again into the workplace during the Second World War and then back into homebody roles afterwards, not all the ground gained was lost. Divorce increased markedly, due in part to the breakdown of marriages undertaken too hastily in wartime or weakened by prolonged separations.

The struggle for equality of pay began with Barbara Castle's Equal Pay Act in 1970. It took a prolonged strike of women machinists making seat covers at the Ford Motor Works to expose the inadequacies of the law that allowed women's work to be almost universally ghettoised and undervalued. Not until 1983, as a result of the Equal Pay (Amendment) Regulations, was equal pay made statutory for work of equal value.

Even before the Sex Discrimination Act of 1975, women had succeeded in achiev-ing some equality for themselves, usually as a result of labour shortages caused by wars or new technology. When wars ended, however, women were either sacked or 'encouraged' to resume their domestic roles to make room for the returning men. When the obvious advantages of hiring deft female fingers or clearly spoken tele-phone operators could no longer be ignored, somehow the work was always down-graded and the pay kept lower than that for a male worker. Frequently 'female' jobs were ghettoised, valued less, and paid less. A man pushing a broom around the floor of a factory on industrial Tyneside in the 1960s would be paid more than his wife, working faster and with more skill on the assembly line.

During the 1960s and 1970s, the contraceptive pill brought more freedom, shotgun marriages became less frequent, and at the same time 'illegitimate' birth began to be less stigmatised. In the latter half of this century one-third of all children are born outside conventional marital relationships and family arrangements can no longer be based on the politicians' rhetoric of the happy nuclear family. There is much talk about children and their need for protection at a time when women are exercising their rights in an unprecedented way, to escape from violent and abusive relationships. For it is women who are instigating the majority of divorces. Probably the most important way society can exercise control of women in the domestic arena is to control the family unit. The nuclear 'family' unit as venerated by the 18-year-long Conservative government is largely irrelevant to the rising number of women in the workplace. Soon there will be more women in work than men, despite the gross lack of support systems; since the Second World War there have never been enough child-care facilities in the workplace for women and their children.

Education is seen as the key to gaining class mobility through changes in employment and women are increasingly gaining higher education qualifications. Even when there is theoretical equality, for instance in access to the national curriculum, there is a 'glass ceiling': women are continually passed over for promotion, even in female-dominated sectors such as teaching, sales or retail. This pattern is replicated throughout society. In neighbourhood supermarkets, for example, women workers and women customers predominate, but the ranks of managers and the seats in the boardroom are dominated by men. Women and ethnic minority candidates have greater difficulty than white male candidates in gaining even the middle ranks of the management ladder, let alone reaching the top. A tiny percentage of company directors in Europe are women; and some of these are working in family-owned companies. Although the situation is changing slowly, largely because of the shrinking number of 'male' jobs and the increasingly large number of 'female' jobs being created, if these jobs remain part-time, undervalued and badly paid, women will still be struggling for real equality.

The appointment of Pauline Clare as the first woman Chief Constable was viewed as tokenistic, despite the fact that she successfully competed against six other candidates for the post. Her previous appointment, as deputy chief constable in Merseyside, followed a sex discrimination complaint brought by Alison Halford, who had been denied the post despite her qualifications. Halford had been attacked through the police canteen grapevine for lesbianism and nymphomania – a typical example of the way women and their actions are disparaged or dismissed in terms of their purported sexual behaviour.

The present trend of employment is to provide the short-term, part-time and low-paid work which women have to settle for, but which men have traditionally not chosen. The closure of the traditional 'heavy' industries such as ship-building, mining and engineering have decimated traditional men's jobs. A young man nowadays, skilled or not, has less chance than his father or even his older brother of finding the kind of work which would allow him to marry and support a family. Economic pressures have long forced women to work outside the home, despite the lack of child-care and the low pay.

## Asian women at work in Britain

On arrival in Britain, Asian women were both affected by and contributed to the change in the position of women. As the post-war boom years ended, cheap labour from the former colonies had to be severely curtailed, culminating in the 1971 Immigration Act. The industrial decline of the early eighties, particularly in the heavy industries of engineering and textiles, had a disproportionate effect on the Asian community. As large numbers of men were compelled to join the ranks of the unemployed, more women had to undertake paid employment to supplement the family income. The technological revolution put an end to heavy manual labour and capital shifted from Europe to the 'Third World' countries to exploit even cheaper labour affecting the Asians living in Britain both socially and economically. The community experienced unemployment at unprecedented levels. In Calderdale, for example, according to the 1991 Census, the unemployment rate among Asian males was 51 per cent as compared with 31 per cent for all males in the area. This has undermined the role of men as the main breadwinners, and women who might not previously have considered paid employment are entering unskilled jobs in assembly or clothing manufacturing, with little job protection. In some instances men go to Europe in search of unskilled work, leaving women behind to look after the family. Asian women's career chances are severely hampered through poor education as the schools they attend are generally under-resourced and the curriculum does nothing to challenge inherent racist ideology. Even the small tokenistic gains made by the anti-racist movement in the 1980s were swept away by the stream of central government controls in education, ostensibly under the banner of improving standards.

Western feminist discourse has largely ignored Asian women's struggle in Britain, just as their efforts in the Subcontinent against British colonialism and exploitation of their labour in factories and elsewhere went largely unnoticed. Their efforts to improve their pay and working conditions, for instance in the Grunwick strike of the 1970s, became worthy of comment, but only to highlight the 'atypical' behaviour of Asian women. In any case it bore no fruit and is relegated to the canons of history – history which is not easily accessible to the next generation of women in general and Asian women in particular.

Women and their work remain undervalued and underpaid. The burden of domestic work usually falls upon women, who therefore seek part-time work; nearly half are part-timers, with consequently fewer opportunities to earn bonuses or overtime, poor promotion prospects, and often without sickness benefit, holiday pay or pension rights. When women succeed in career terms they are seen as atypical or not endowed with the 'real' qualities of femininity.

When an Asian woman is employed, she may be subject to more subtle discrimination; being seen as conforming or not conforming to a stereotype imposed on her by the society in which she is working. Mittsuye Yamada describes the no-win situation:

> ... an Asian American woman thriving under the smug illusion that I was *not* the stereotypic image of the Asian woman because I had a career teaching English in a community college. I did not think anything assertive was necessary to make my point ... it was so much my expected role that it ultimately rendered me invisible ... contrary to what I thought, I had actually been contributing to my own stereotyping ... When the Asian American woman is lulled into believing that people perceive her as being different from other Asian women (the submissive, subservient, ready-to-please, easy-to-get-along-with Asian woman), she is kept comfortably content with the state of things (Trinh,1989).

## Media Treatment of Asian Women

The headline **Asian Woman Killed For 'Having Affair'** (*Guardian*, 26 September 1995), roused a great deal of comment, informed and otherwise. Would a man in a similar situation have suffered the same fate? Or does the 'honour' of the family rest only on the sexual behaviour of the female? The woman, Tasleem Sadiq, was a young British-raised divorcee of Asian Pakistani origin, murdered by her brother-in-law who repeatedly ran over her with a car because of her affair with a married man.

The media treatment of this case, like the reporting of the death by sati of Roop Kanwar in India, illustrates how forces of patriarchy and neo-colonialism work against Asian women whereever they live. The Sadiq case caused such a sensation that 'experts' on Islam, Muslim and non-Muslim, were called on to make pronouncements as to whether so-called 'honour killing' is Islamic ('Sunday' programme, BBC Radio 4, 1 October 1995). On the same day, and on the same radio network, there was coverage of child sex abuse cases brought against several members of the Roman Catholic hierarchy in Ireland – but no committee of 'experts' on Christianity was summoned to ascertain the legitimacy or otherwise of this type of transgression according to Biblical sources.

Immigrants sometimes experience a disconcerting gap between the familiar culture they left and the state to which it has evolved when they return on visits. Immigrant communities in general reminisce about the past, especially if things in the adopted country do not come up to expectation. The Asian community is no different: they dream of a non-existent golden age they left behind and to which they will one day return. Similarly, when parents want their children to adopt a philosophy different from that of the majority community, they may exaggerate the standards they expect of them in the hope that it may deter the children from being too absorbed into the dominant culture. Parents arrange for their children to attend supplementary schools in religio-cultural instruction and community languages. Again, this is a well-established pattern of immigrant communities. So is the tradition of arranging marriages with partners from the country of origin to cement familiar and cultural relationships.

This process of cultural change is not linear or one-dimensional. In Hegelian terms, when there is a thesis and anti-thesis, their collision is inevitable and may produce synthesis. Synthesis of a new culture taking from the new and the old. This cultural synthesis is at an individual and community level and has interesting and intricate dynamics. House furniture and furnishings, food, music and dress, all bear witness to the interplay between different forces brought to bear on the lives of Asians in Britain. Asians absorb aspects of Western culture but they also influence it. Not only has the classical music of raga or *quwali* become accessible to mainstream society but *bhangra* and blues are now combining the two musical traditions. Words like *chumcha* and *fatwa* have become useable currency since the Salman Rushdie affair. Language, like other social tools, is adapted for particular use and ease. Asians at home may use a mixture of sentence structure and vocabulary, weaving in and out of standard English and one or more Asian language.

Asian women growing up in Britain are continuing to carve out a role and identity for themselves against a barrage of pressures from various societal sources including the educational system. An Asian woman may select aspects of Asian culture to suit her needs that are quite different from – even in conflict with – those of her parents. Similarly the aspects of Western culture she chooses may be at variance with the values the educational system wishes to inculcate. The synthesis of a new culture operates at both an individual and community level and is further coloured by the class position of the individual and her family. For example, a woman may live a high-tech life complete with the internet, microwave, a chauffeur-driven car and wear a headcovering as a declaration of her Muslim or Sikh identity. Whilst she may be trying to establish her identity in Britain by covering her head, her counter-parts in the Subcontinent may be moving in the opposite direction, and for much the same reasons. A British Asian university student may simultaneously be wearing *hejjab* and Doc Martens. She may choose to accept a marriage partner selected by her parents from the Subcontinent. Conversely, she could be quite conservative in her thinking and yet marry outside her religious, social or racial group.

Given their disparate cultural, religious, linguistic, geographical, socio-economic and educational backgrounds, the notion of the 'Asian woman' becomes a spurious label. She could be an aristocrat, an accomplished musician or a scientist; she could be a singer, an actress, a journalist, a political activist, a doctor, a factory worker or a housewife. She could be married, single or divorced; have children or not. She could have complete control over considerable income of her own or others, whether or not in paid work; she could own property, live in rented accommodation, or have no resources of any kind. She could be liberal or conservative, reactionary or revolutionary. She could be religious, atheist or agnostic; monotheist or poly-theist. She could be vegetarian or omnivorous; she may avoid eating certain meats, or keep Islamic food laws. She could be highly political or apolitical; parochial, communist, capitalist, nationalist, internationalist. She could be an immigrant, or born in Britain either of mixed parentage or to parents whose family origins are in the Subcontinent but who were born elsewhere. The Asian woman living in Britain or in the country of origin does not live in a cultural vacuum. National and inter-national events impinge on and shape her life. But she continues to be viewed by the institutions in Britain as a victim of a backward and barbaric culture whose salvation lies in the hands of the white man and whose family is the agent of her oppression.

## Case study: Asian women's experience in an English town

Wings clipped,
we struggle to fly.
With trust betrayed
we're locked and caged.

The case study which follows is informed by my personal experience, firstly of growing up in Britain as an immigrant myself, one of the first wave of Asian women to pass through the British higher education system and secondly of working in the field of education for twenty years. The formal interviews presented here were gathered over several years while I was an education officer in Calderdale and Leeds. All the names of interviewees are fictitious.

Between September 1993 and October 1995, I was assigned the task of conducting action research to examine the effectiveness of projects in Calderdale's education department – commonly referred to as 'Section 11' projects because they were funded by the Home Office under Section 11 of the Local Government Act 1966 – and to elicit the views of the local Asian community about their educational achievements, the effectiveness of education provision and how it might be improved.

The women I interviewed ranged in age from sixteen to sixty. As with the Sub-continent research, the interviews were arranged through people I knew. Over the period I had been working in Calderdale, beginning in 1988, my relationships with many Asian women had developed beyond the purely professional. By the time of the interviews in 1995-6, many of these relationships were based on trust, so the women felt able to divulge personal information which they might have been hesi-tant to disclose under normal circumstances.

Like the women in the Subcontinent, they were keen to know about the outcome of the research project. Many had had experience of local education authority surveys which were little more than paper exercises. Although they were sceptical of the outcome of my project, they were prepared to give me their most precious commodity – time. The interviews ranged from thirty minutes, sandwiched between busy training schedules or housework chores, to leisurely chats in the comfort of homes over cups of tea or a meal. Group interviews took several hours.

Asian women, this book has related, have come to Britain from varied socio-economic, religio-linguistic and political backgrounds. Some came from the upper leisured classes: they dressed in imported finery, played musical instruments, read romantic novels, organised their servants and their household and occasionally turned their hand to cooking. Their conversation with other women revolved round films or shows they might have seen, the latest fashion in clothes, jewellery, hair styles or furnishings and dinner parties, and the dowries they were preparing for their children when they got married after they left their Swiss boarding schools.

There was another group of immigrants, much like the women in Meena Bazaar and the teachers in Karachi, who had been working in 'respectable' careers to contribute to the family budget or to finance their own or others' education or pay for luxuries. Many were hard-headed business or professional women, accustomed to running businesses or schools. A third group, like women in the clothing factory in Karachi, had no formal marketable skills but had been driven to work by force of circumstance. The fourth were the social 'untouchables', carrying out the most menial of all jobs: sweeping and cleaning public toilets. Some were from the *Harajin* caste of Hindus, others from other religious groups.

What all shared was a belief that they were coming to a free and fair society in which they would be treated equally, irrespective of their class or religious background. For many, coming to England was a liberation from the old order: the new world generated hope that the traditional ways of doing things could be cast off and experimenting with the new, unfamiliar and daring could begin. There was little if any understanding or anticipation of the all-pervasive British class system, or of the fact that gender-differentiation was just as strong in Britain as at home.

Adjustments to the new world took many forms. Strict observance of purdah was abandoned. Many middle-class women who had left their *burquas* at Lahore or Mombasa airports were seen sharing a dinner table with their white male and female neighbours and friends or seated on the bus beside a strange man. They began to learn English through volunteer English as a second language (ESL) schemes and to try English food and clothes, especially trouser suits when they became fashionable in the late sixties. They began to exchange cooking recipes and styles of dress with women from different parts of the Subcontinent. The habit of wearing heavily decorated clothing became rare, as – for a time – did the custom of giving dowries. Simple marriages, some arranged on the telephone with partners in the Subcontinent, began to be contracted. The community was robust and energetic in its belief that with hard work all was possible. Mastering the English language and familiarity with the local customs were often seen as the key to unlimited success. Parents ensured that their children were fluent in English and began to adopt local customs such as birthday parties and Christmas celebrations. A number allowed their daughters to wear school uniform without any reference to *shalwar* or *hejjab*. Thus began the new social and cultural experiment.

In the late 1960s, through a mixture of local and central government funding, community relations organisations were set up to facilitate the mixing of different cultural groups. There was a general belief that ignorance about one another's cultures was at the root of racial prejudice, which could thus be overcome through education and familiarity. However, whilst friendships were indeed developed at individual level, British institutions and officialdom were seldom neutral. They were at best indifferent and often hostile, as indicated by the treatment meted out to Asians in terms of both service provision and employment opportunities.

Places of worship and community centres invariably became the forum for Asian men to vent their frustrated professional and political ambitions. These were often conservative and reactionary institutions, which excluded women from the decision making processes. As these bodies became the sounding-boards of community opinion, they excluded Asian women and their aspirations from the agenda. Just as sati and purdah had been justified during the colonial period on religious grounds, so denying women a full part in the socio-economic and political life of the Subcontinent, so the pattern began to be repeated in Britain. Local and national politicians, mostly men, began to negotiate with Asian men in their temples; and the absence of women was explained – if the subject arose at all – as simply part of the Asian cultural or religious background. Just as once puppet rulers sympathetic to the ideals of the Raj had been installed in the Subcontinent, so the so-called 'community leaders' who could be relied on not to challenge authority, were patronised by the authorities as a means of maintaining the status quo and effectively stifling community development.

One of the earliest signs that things were amiss with the dream of a new life in Britain was manifest in the education service. Parents who had high hopes for their daughters' education and respect for their teachers found their academically able daughters being channelled into non-academic courses and advised to pursue careers which were less demanding than their ability warranted. Zakia, one of the women I interviewed in a northern English town, came from an urban middle-class background in Pakistan. Her parents wanted her to go to university, as did she from the age of eleven, and they ensured that she went to a school which catered for her educational needs. Although she had worn *burqua* in Pakistan from the age of twelve, which was the custom at the time for girls of her age and class, within a year of coming to England in 1964 in her mid-teens, she wore a skirt to school in order to integrate into the new social surroundings. Within three years she had sufficient command of English to pass her 'O' levels and proceed to 'A' levels; she was amongst the few in her year to be studying for four 'A' levels and one of the handful wanting to go to university.

Zakia described the scene when the careers teacher came to discuss their choices with the class:

> She breezed in, sat down and looked down her list of names. My name was on top of the list of university candidates. She looked up and said, 'Universities: Zakia Malik.' There was one of those condescending pauses. Then: 'And where is our ambitious Zakia?' I thought to myself 'Sod you woman. I'll get to university if it kills me.' And I did.

Such attitudes have persisted, despite the efforts of a number of committed white educationalists. Twenty years later, Cecile Wright (in Eggleston, 1986) noted:

> The attitude of teachers to... Asian cultures is at worst negative and at best condescending and patronising. ...Pupils are seen as recipients, with very little to offer to the curriculum. Teachers view themselves as doing a good job by educating 'these immigrants' in the 'best education system in the world'.

Zakia subsequently became a teacher, but she continued to find herself in marginal positions (the so-called 'multicultural' education posts with a glass ceiling of middle management) whilst her white, especially male, colleagues continued to climb the professional ladder. When she tried to improve employment opportunities and service delivery for ethnic minorities – the job she was employed to do – she found herself further alienated from her white colleagues.

Asian women in other areas of Britain shared a similar fate: highly educated and skilled women found themselves forced to take jobs which were far below their ability and experience, as their qualifications were frequently not recognised for their true value. The virtual absence of Asians from key professions became a matter of concern for the communities themselves and for white liberals. The frustration over widespread racial discrimination spilled into the streets of Britain in 1981 in the form of violent urban disturbances. As a consequence, official policy on race relations began to be reconsidered. Asian women, for their part, also began to reconsider their relationship with their adopted country. They began to highlight the need for separate space for themselves in which they could define their own identities and requirements. From the mid-eighties a few schemes were set up for unemployed Asian women, financed through the European Social Fund. A small minority of Asian women reached the ranks of middle management in the 'multicultural' areas in LEAs and other public sectors.

Another consequence of the new policies was the emergence of a sprinkling of Asian 'community leaders' – some of the same men who had risen to prominence in the temples – as elected representatives and as local authority employees in race-related jobs. This process of allowing space for the voice of the Asian community created an illusion of involvement and power, jealously guarded by those in post, who were almost without exception men.

When the authorities made these appointments, class differences within the Asian communities were ignored; it was assumed that one Asian was much the same as another, and that they would automatically relate to other members of that community.

The few women employed in the public sector often found themselves professionally frustrated, as the jobs available did not correspond to their educational training and they were compelled to work in fields for which they had no understanding or empathy. So these employment practices, which echoed education's 'sari, samosa and steel band' syndrome, were – and continue to be – tokenist. The basic structural inequities were left unchallenged.

The case of another woman I interviewed illustrates how the forces of patriarchy and colonial attitudes in British institutions continue to affect the life choices of Asian women in Britain. Sophia, in her mid-thirties, was born in the Mirpur area of Pakistan. She came to England when she was a toddler and had all her schooling in England. She gained several 'O' levels and an 'A' level in Art and Design. As a result of her portfolio she secured a place at a prestigious American fashion school in London with the possibility of studying in America. She was unable to take up her place, however, because she was not informed that there were Discretionary Awards for non-graduate courses, and was advised against her decision by a careers teacher who assured her that fashion and design was a 'no go' area for Asian women.

Sophia's subsequent experiences are of interest. In the following years she married and had four children, and continued to pursue a career as a community artist, designing clothes and batik. She was one of the workers in a voluntary sector project funded through the European Social Fund as a means of teaching dress-making skills to unemployed Asian women. This funding eventually ran out and the scheme was taken over by the borough council with a reduced budget and staffing, until its eventual withdrawal in 1995. Each time the project was threatened, Sophia mobilised local people to lobby various council committees in order to save it, and attracted much media attention.

She remained undeterred by the final withdrawal of funds. Her determination to see the work of the organisation continue was such that she bought a disused working men's club and, with the help of funds raised through a mixture of voluntary and statutory bodies and the practical efforts of her husband, managed to resume her work as a community artist as she settled into her career. 'The council treated us badly over the years,' she told me. 'If they think we're dead, I'll show them. Over my dead body!'

Although Sophia had some sympathy for an advice centre run by one of the Asian male elected members of the local authority, she was highly critical of the authority's role in giving priority to male-run projects such as the Racial Equality Council, formerly the Community Relations Council, over a women's organisation. The final funding blow to her organisation came as a result of criticism by the local authority and Asian men's organisations of the women's work as incompetent and, worse still, disreputable because their advice on individual rights was breaking up families. Sophia wanted her eleven year old daughter to have a better formal education than she did and to become a teacher.

It was clear by the mid-eighties that the multicultural/anti-racist era triggered by the 1981 events (Scarman, 1981) had failed to address the most fundamental problems. Notable educationalists such as Madan Sarup were beginning to ask serious questions. Sarup (1986) commented that Britain was:

> ... undergoing a political and economic crisis. But it is also a crisis of the whole culture, of the society's sense of itself. The issue of race provides one of the most important ways of understanding how this society actually works and how it has arrived where it is.

> Asian pupils are on the edges of socio-economic and cultural life in Britain. This dismissal to the periphery is a generalised experience which constitutes a new and inferior form of citizenship, what Rushdie (1980) called the new empire in Britain.

Poor educational achievement by Asian pupils tends to bolster white illusions of linguistic and cultural superiority and to absolve educators of their responsibility to offer an equitable education to all. The educational system in Britain reproduces values with which Asians often do not identify. Woven into the very fabric of British educational thinking is a notion of white racial and cultural superiority, constantly refined to suit the particular situation, which Asians frequently internalise. For example, because their languages are denied their rightful place in the educational system, not only are Asians being cut off from their roots in past history but their future development is also retarded. Asian girls whose view of the world is expressed in their language, religion and clothing have no official place in the world of education; this can cause them stress and undermine their self-confidence, which may in turn alienate them from pursuing education and career (Crishna, 1975). The stress and confusion is increased by the continual mismatch between the rhetoric of the education system and society and their own experience of racism and racial harassment in education and in the workplace.

The education of Asian students in general and women in particular remains a peripheral issue in the world of education and politics. The issue fails to secure the support of Asian parents generally, and political parties pay it no attention. On the contrary, to make a stand on 'race' is seen as a vote loser: the complete absence of Asian women from parliament and large sections of public life is never raised. Just as it was once thought that the 'darker' races were not fit to rule themselves – thus justifying European colonialism – so in Britain Asian culture is perceived to be responsible for the plight of its women. The white man's (or white woman's) burden still remains the same: to rescue Asian women from their backward culture and superstitious and/or aggressive religion. The 'rescued' Asian woman wears Western clothes, speaks English to the exclusion of Asian languages and has a belief in Western-type democracy and the so-called freedom of the individual.

Asian women's struggle in Britain, on the picket lines (1996), through the courts and in more subtle ways within the institutions in which they work, appears to have produced no real change. They invariably remain on the margins of their professions even if they are successful in gaining training and employment in their chosen careers. As the community has become more disenchanted with Britain it has begun to become as self-sufficient as it can. Women's role as custodians of culture has been central to this shift, particularly concentrated in familial relations. In the face of endemic racial discrimination in British society, Asian men have come to look to their women for support and affirmation in an unprecedented way. Many Asian women accept this, even when it means tolerating sexism and assuming roles which sit uncomfortably with their own interests, so as to stand up to the threat from the world outside. This is no different from the behaviour of any group which perceives itself to be under attack from an external force. For instance, during wars, class difference and other personal issues in Britain have always been subordinated to nationalism, to the greater cause of fighting the common enemy.

Women's dress, as discussed earlier, is a telling example: on social occasions such as weddings, it is extremely rare nowadays for women to wear anything other than clothing styles from the Subcontinent. The latest fashions in clothes and jewellery are transported from Karachi or Bombay to the streets of Leeds or London. In many instances Asian women make special trips to the Subcontinent to replenish their wardrobes and prepare dowries for their children – which are becoming ever more costly and elaborate (see Menski, 1998).

Supplementary schools have come into their own as bastions of cultural identity for children who are becoming alienated by the state educational system. The values and pedagogy of such institutions are often at variance with mainstream schools, as teachers there either hold no formal training or are trained overseas and have different teaching styles. One of the most important functions they serve is self-determination for a community otherwise disempowered from fully participating in the life of society. Here, unlike in the state school system, there is full agreement between the parents and teachers on the mode of dress, school ethos and curriculum. For example, school-age Muslim girls who normally wear Western-style school uniform can be seen after school wearing *shalwar qumeez* and *hejjab,* clutching their Quran on their way to the *muddrassah* or Mosque school. The whole etiquette of gaining command of a text written in Arabic – which is not their mother tongue – is taken as seriously by parents as by students. There may be different rates of progress, but the vast majority of pupils achieve the goal. Some schools also concentrate on teaching Urdu, the state language of Pakistan and the lingua franca in the Subcontinent before the partition – and again, this is not the first language of most Muslim children in Britain. A similar pattern emerges in the Hindu and Sikh communities. This is in sharp contrast to the lack of communication between parents and schools in the mainstream system, as discussed later in this chapter.

Some Asian women have taken to adopting a strict code of religio-cultural conduct. For example, Sharifa came to Britain as a baby and had all her education in England, culminating in a degree in English and Arabic. She decided to have an arranged marriage with a cousin from Pakistan because she felt that that would enable her to be in better touch with her religio-cultural roots. Her husband was enterprising and found a job working in a fashion shop but Sharifa remained the main breadwinner, working in 'equal opportunities'. She has three children and when her eldest daughter was coming up to the age of eleven she decided to do a Postgraduate Certificate in Education (PGCE) and get a job as a teacher in the local Muslim girls' school where she planned to send her daughter. She felt that the Islamic environment of the school, where she could wear the full *hejjab,* best served their religious needs and reinforced their true identity. She felt that the multicultural experience had gone too far and did not want to take chances with her children. Interestingly, she believed that European and other converts to Islam were the true light to Asian Muslims, who had somehow lost their way through being in the Subcontinent for over a thousand years. Similar sentiments are expressed by the Hindu and Sikh communities about their religions being diluted by mixing with Muslims.

We have seen how Asian girls are consistently encouraged to follow courses in mainstream education which are seen as 'soft' options and do not lead to professional careers. If girls wish to pursue a professional route they take longer to gain the required academic qualifications. They continue to be stereotyped as non-achievers both educationally and in career terms. They have been perceived by teachers as not regarding education as important in itself or as a route to worthwhile occupations. As yet there has been no meaningful dialogue between parents and teachers which might disabuse teachers of these views. The wearing of *shalwar qumeez* to school has provoked much comment, but no quantifiable research on its effect on educational achievement. However, it further distinguishes Asian girls as 'different' and many white teachers hold negative views about such clothes' suitability for school. As late as 1995, the Higher Education Funding Council on Special Initiatives to Encourage Widening Participation of Students from Ethnic Minorities in Teacher Training reported that 'one project quoted an example of an Asian student who was told not to wear a sari to school by a local authority adviser'. Women all over the Subcontinent wear *shalwar qumeez* and saris. Their achievement is not hampered by their clothing – some even become Prime Ministers.

Asian students going through the British educational system are generally led to believe that people in the Subcontinent live in makeshift dwellings and the girls have no educational or career chances. For example, a group of girls from a secondary school in Bradford who visited Islamabad on a school exchange were 'bowled over by the sophistication and liberation of their counterparts'. The girls thought that 'people in Pakistan would live in mud huts and would never let their daughters out alone'. 'We went out there thinking that Pakistan was a developing country, but we found it was so advanced. The girls were all really hard-working and wanted to be doctors or teachers. Their parents were ambitious for their daughters. We ended up thinking it was Bradford that was backward' (*Bradford Telegraph and Argus*, 6 July 1995).

Social class differences among Asians have not been significantly ameliorated by their move to Britain, nor by the fact that second and third generation children have been exposed to English language and culture from birth. There is some evidence to suggest a link between social origin and areas of settlement in Britain, with, for example, unskilled labourers concentrated in the textile industry areas in the north of England. These were precisely the regions most vulnerable to unemployment in the post-technological revolution, hence perpetuating the cycle of disadvantage.

A 1993 investigation into education provision in Calderdale for Asian females aged over 16 by community worker, Naseem Aqeel (1995), highlights the relationship between gender, race and class. The 43 girls involved were based in one of the local secondary schools located in the 'inner ring' area of Halifax.

All had extremely low expectations, despite their good examination results in some cases. Many, however, lacked basic literacy skills. This contrasted with the study carried out in Karachi, discussed in Chapter 4, in which Asian young women were shown to have high expectations of educational attainment and career possibilities. The fundamental difference appears to be that the parents and teachers of the young women in Karachi neither doubted nor undermined their ability. If families could not afford to finance the education of their daughters, or if the young women wanted financial independence, there was at least one 'safe' place – the Meena Bazaar. There is no such equivalent in the British context.

None of the girls interviewed by Aqeel (1995) had received any detailed individual guidance; they were reluctant to articulate their own needs, including those regarding education; they revealed low levels of confidence and self-esteem. This may be due to the absence of positive role models and the inappropriateness of the curriculum.

The vast majority of parents, themselves not educated in Britain, understood little about their children's education, and could not make up for the lack of careers guidance from the professional careers officers and teachers. Most Asian girls had set their career boundaries at clerical, secretarial, or care work. Even the choice of sixth form over further education college was primarily influenced by the negative views of the college held by parents and community. This appears to be a general pattern which further curtails women's educational chances of progress. Such paucity of parental involvement and information is confirmed by a young man I interviewed in Calderdale in connection with the local education authority's education provision for the Asian community. He said:

> All they (his parents) knew was our son's going to school and coming back at three o'clock – that's all they knew. They didn't know what he was doing at school, how many subjects. Parents should be more involved in school and interpreters provided.

Another said: 'All parents knew was to take the children to school and get the tea ready'. It was apparent that parents of the people interviewed were keen for their children to succeed, but did not know how to help them other than by arranging for private tuition, which they did.

## Interviews with women in Calderdale

The first interview, with three women, is informative in two ways: firstly, in revealing the different attitudes to and experiences of the educational system dependent upon the women's class position (the middle-class women laid greater emphasis on family discipline which found expression in both the mother and daughter-in-law wearing the *hejjab*); and secondly, in showing that the effect of racism in employment transcended class divisions.

Radia and Zainib had come to Britain over two decades ago. Radia's daughter-in-law Jameela was a recent arrival. All have children. Radia is a housewife. Zainib was employed in a garment factory and Jameela was undergoing training at the Calderdale Community Training Centre. All three were educated in Pakistan. Radia had a university degree; Zainib had passed her school-leaving examination (matriculation); and Jameela had completed her university entrance examination.

Radia made much of her educated middle-class background and the fact that her husband worked for the local authority. This, she believed, enabled her to make the right choices for her children's education. One of her children went to the local grammar school but she understood (wrongly) that it had become a comprehensive school, and so standards had dropped. When asked why she thought so, she said that on amalgamation of this grammar school with another, which she believed to be inferior, 'the children from the school with the lower standard are mixed in with them, in so doing cannot attain a high standard of education. Because of this we decided to send him to a private school.' This private school was the Bradford Grammar School, of which she had received good reports from friends who sent their sons there. She also felt that if there were too many Asian pupils in a given school, teachers paid them less attention and exhibited racist behaviour. When asked if the private schools were free from racism, she said, 'No, it does exist, but it depends on the family background. Some people blame teachers, but it also depends upon the girls and boys. I've never experienced it myself, nor have my children, but it does happen a little bit.'

She believed that the child's own interest in education, as well as the company they keep, is as important as the quality of schooling. 'Our children do not go out, we haven't controlled them that much, but the home environment is such that they don't go out'. At this, Zainib commented, 'Children are children, of course, and they should have time to play out.'

Radia:      Children are children, I'm not saying...

Zainib:     Home background! No parents want their child to be 'wrong!'

Radia:      Yes, yes, no parent wants....

Zainib:     She is educated. (Pointing to Radia) I only did Matric Pakistan, as did my husband, but we wanted our children to be educated so that they wouldn't be like us, do you understand?

Radia:      That's right. We also thought....

Zainib:     No, you said because you were educated... We didn't even know that there was such a thing as the 11 plus. Even so, we did what we could for our children. The first two children were helped at home and we arranged private tuition for the third.

Radia:      Listen. Don't be offended by what I said about the home background having importance... It doesn't mean your home background is no good. I'm not saying this no, no, no.

Zainib:     Even though the older two did not go to the Grammar School, they have still done well. The eldest daughter was one of the Training Officers at Calderdale Training Centre and the son had some other responsible position.

Radia:     Look, if a child is studious it will succeed, even in ordinary Secondary School.

Zainib:    When there are more Asian children in school the teachers do not give them much attention and put all the blame on our children (pointing to Radia) and this lady says that she has never had complaints from the teachers.

Radia:     Now if you go to this...school, (referring to the local former secondary modern school which had only recently acquired comprehensive status) there isn't a single English child. Where there are no English pupils, how will English teachers pay attention to them? They will never do it.

Note:      'Matric Pakistan' is a secondary school leaving examination taken in Pakistan.

The '11 plus' was a competitive examination taken at the age of 11 for entry into the selective school system in England.

Radia went on to say that at this school with its many Asian pupils, the white parents took their children away. This was a retrograde step and should not happen. The teachers should continue to give the same attention to their Asian pupils as to their white pupils: 'I think both teachers and pupils should be really mixed, i.e. representative of the community'.

This interview highlighted some fascinating community dynamics and pointed to the dangers of reaching for simple off-the-peg solutions to complex issues. What is very clear is that the families' own financial and educational backgrounds have a bearing on educational aspirations and outcomes, which in turn affect the parents' and perhaps the children's own attitudes towards the teachers and the educational system. The positive attitudes of parents and educational successes of students do not necessarily translate into reality in the world of work. Radia's son, despite his private school and university degree in Biomedicine, had been unable to find employment in his field for a whole year. He was retraining as a dentist. The daughter had been to the local grammar school and both boys to Bradford Grammar School. The daughter was at Manchester University in her final year. Zainib's lack of knowledge about the 11-plus did not deter her from ensuring that her children received the best education available. In another interview with her son, it transpired that she had accompanied him to Pakistan for a 'good' education when he was facing racist abuse at school from other pupils and was unsupported by the school. Her observation about the teachers' expectation of Asian students and the 'white flight' were very perceptive. She also recognised that Asian pupils' acquisition of English will be impeded by the absence of native speakers of English. What is also illuminating is their ideal model of a 'good' education: one which is representative of the population it serves, in both curricular and employment terms.

Radia was keen to insist that parents must ensure that their children know their linguistic and religious roots. She emphasised the need for children to go to the mosque and for Muslim women to wear the *hejjab*, as she and her daughter-in-law did.

The subject of the next interview was born in a Punjabi village in India. Sutbir had an English-medium boarding-school education in Shimla. Arriving in England in her late teens, she studied for 'A' level university entrance examination and read English at university. With an upper second-class degree and a diploma in further education, she sought a teaching career in a further education college, for which she was amply qualified.

> After numerous unsuccessful applications I thought: these gorey (white people) are never going to give me a job teaching English. So I decided to trek the race relations path. And that's where I've been ever since. Well, that's not easy either.

When I interviewed her in 1995, she had two part-time jobs: one at a community centre and the other at a university. Both were short-term contracts. The former ended due to the local authority's withdrawal of funds, the latter she lost when the permanent job on the degree course in Black Women's literature that she had established was given to a white academic.

> There is nowhere for us to go. We can't even succeed in our own area. As Asian women we have no-one to talk to and no-one to look up to. The whites're expert on us, and that's that.

She was not to be beaten by this experience, and finally obtained a multicultural education post in the education department of a Local Education Authority in another locality.

Salma, the next interviewee, came from an upper middle-class family in Pakistan. Her family had a long political and diplomatic history before and after partition. After several disappointments on the career front in England, she pursued a Postgraduate Certificate in Education for overseas graduates at a local higher education institution. She was unable to secure a post in the area of her training and has since decided to do a degree in information technology.

The fifth interview was with a group of nine women. All except one were born in the Mirpur area of Azad Kashmir in Pakistan and spoke little or no English. All lived in an area with multiple disadvantages including high unemployment and poor housing. Eight were married with children. All lived on tight budgets because their husbands, who had once worked in the local woollen mills, were now un-employed. None worked outside the home; most did not have marketable skills to supplement the family budget. A couple took in sewing from neighbours or friends. Despite their class position and financial state, they all valued education for their children. Many saved from their meagre income to pay for private tuition for their children in their weakest subjects. Most relied on support and advice from the community itself in choosing education courses and career paths. Most expressed dissatisfaction with the education system and careers advice provided to their children, and their allocation to schools.

The sixth group of interviewees were all trainees at Calderdale Community Training Centre. Their responses can be summed up in tabular form:

| Question | Response |
|---|---|
| What is my situation? | Two in the Sixth form at local grammar school. Three on training programme to improve their English and office skills. |
| What have I done to help myelf? | Attend work experience placement at Community Centre. Attend courses at Community Centre. Attend courses at College. |
| What are the barriers to my success? | Provision in mainstream education often limited and less flexible in meeting the needs of Asian women. |
| What would I like in an ideal community situation? | Positive role models and community language provision in the education system. |

Of the five women, two were at the local grant maintained school on work experience for a few weeks. The rest were following a training programme which combined English as a Second Language (ESL) with computer studies and other office skills. Their routes to the centre were varied. Lakbir, for example, had been employed in an electronics firm in London. When she moved to Halifax, she searched the job market but found nothing. Through her visits to the Job Centre, she was referred to the training organisation. She wanted to learn basic computing skills and enough English to obtain employment.

Sadia and Nabila were each studying for three 'A' levels. Sadia was doing a project on archaeology in the Sixth form, for which she had gathered material from various universities including Bradford, where she eventually hoped to read Archaeology. She was also learning computer studies in the holidays and during her placement at the training centre. Her main reason for going there was to be in touch with her community, to which she hoped to contribute when she qualified. Miryam and Syria learned about the course from their husbands. This was interesting as the professional view is that Asian men do not want their women to attend courses. The reason for their attending the centre were three-fold: English as a Second Language provision, créche facilities and bilingual teachers. Syria had attended classes provided by the local education authority (LEA) for six weeks, but found that she was given twice the time at the centre she received at the LEA Adult Education classes. And she could question the tutors in her mother tongue when she did not understand something. There was a discussion on the pros and cons of bilingual teachers in ESL provision. Miryam and Syria felt that bilingual strategies were effective because they made meaning immediately accessible. Lakbir felt that whilst there was merit in the use of mother tongue in teaching ESL the students might become lazy if they always relied on the teacher to explain things in the first language rather than piece together the meaning for themselves from the context.

They had different reasons for learning English. Lakbir wanted to secure employment similar to her London job. Syria wanted to be an independent housewife, able, for example, to go to the doctor or do her shopping satisfactorily. Miryam had studied English in Pakistan and wanted to improve it in order to study to become a teacher. She was studying for General Certificate in Secondary Education examinations (GCSEs) at the local college.

All five women had taken positive steps to help themselves to shape their futures. The two schoolgirls wanted to learn more about the community they had come from as well as contribute to it. Two had come to learn English to enhance their educational and employment prospects, one to improve her social life, two as part of their community studies programme.

The final three interviewees were attending various activities at the Asian Women's Resource Association (AWRA). The answers to my questions appear below. The voluntary organisation AWRA included amongst its repertoire of courses keep-fit,

| Question | Response |
|---|---|
| What is my situation? | Formal education ranged from GCSE to 'A' Level standard. |
| What have I done to help myself? | Ranged from part-time to full-time employment, Youth and Community Work qualification, short courses at AWRA, part-time Cert. for mature students to gain entry to B.Ed. |
| What are the barriers to my success? | Lack of information on grants, inadequate course/careers counselling. Lack of child care provision. Lack of role models. Inappropriate curriculum. |
| What would I like in an ideal community situation? | Better child care provision, classes between 9am – 3pm, better career/course counselling, appropriate curriculum, culturally relevant models. |

child-care, English for Speakers of Other Languages, Fashion and Design, Desktop Publishing, Textiles, Urdu, Personal Effectiveness, counselling, advice, and training for volunteers. AWRA was very popular among Asian women as it was the only organisation specifically tailored to their needs.

Nabeela was married with one child. She had started at General National Vocational Qualification level three at the local college but had had to give up because her daughter 'kept falling ill.' She said that, 'to take time out for yourself gets harder when you've children.' Adequate childcare would have solved her problem. The lack of child-care facilities was still not resolved, but the generally supportive environment of AWRA enabled her simultaneously to mind her daughter and pursue courses in fashion and design, batik, textiles and basic level Urdu.

She was in support of a more flexible approach to learning: lessons should start after the children had gone to school and in places less daunting than the formal setting of a college. From that point of view AWRA was ideal. Commenting on schools, she said: 'Nurseries and schools are not bothered about a child's education. They need to encourage the child.' She went on to say that the child's own background should be reflected in the school curriculum. For example, GCSE in needlecraft should include making Asian clothes and not simply have Western styles imposed on everyone. An educational system needs to have an environment which is conducive to learning, and this can only happen when teachers understand their pupils. This should go hand in glove with an interesting and energising curriculum. Children are more likely to respond when their imaginations are kindled than if forced to learn. She advocated a lifelong learning programme for members of the community, especially those who did not have a chance the first time round. Many parents, she thought, could not afford to have their children in full-time formal education:

> In many instances parents can not afford to have their children at school and are tantalised by the prospect of an allowance on the Youth Training Scheme, but these short term measures have a bleak future as they do not have accredited qualifications, nor do they lead to employment. In short a waste of time.

Kulsoom left school with five GCSEs and two 16+ passes. She wanted to go to university, so needed 'A' levels, but her programme was halted because she had married, and she needed to be in paid employment to bring her husband from Pakistan. She was studying for the Certificate for Mature Students, which would qualify her for a B.Ed course. Although she had found her college tutor helpful on course and career advice, she wanted better counselling for Asian women caught between immigration laws governing their partners' entry into Britain and their education. She emphasised the need for a more balanced curriculum at all levels of education. 'There may be the odd Urdu lesson, otherwise it's all theirs (white people's). From day one everything is about them. Even RE is about Christianity.' She emphasised the need for Asian professionals in key positions in the education service, not just as non-teaching assistants. She thought that the white teachers lacked understanding about their Asian students and that non-teaching assistants and classroom assistants did not know enough about the National Curriculum to help the students.

What was abundantly clear from all the interviews was that the limitations on the career and employment outcomes are more a reflection of inappropriate careers advice, lack of financial support and general counselling, and inappropriate curriculum, than of any lack of interest in either education or career progression on the part of Asian women and their parents.

An Asian child on entry to school is fluent in at least one language and often more, but after eleven years of schooling remains confident in none. Asian girls enter school with a sense of who they are but their confidence in their cultural heritage is undermined by the educational system. As George Orwell's character in *Burmese Days* observed, Asians were taught to 'drink whisky and play football... but precious little else' (Orwell, 1958). Asian women are taught to speak English after a fashion and aspire to Western cultural values, but little else. Their search for a good standard of education, employment and promotion within the professions, especially the world of education, remains elusive.

The lack of choices for Asian women in education is reflected throughout every area of public life in Britain. Take health care as an example, where Asian women are conspicuous by their absence. White men hold the power in the National Health Service (NHS) and are able to exert pressure on policies which work to their advantage. This is compounded by the typecasting of Asian women as ignorant, unable even to speak English, and the consequent assumption that they cannot make informed decisions about their health. Hence they are effectively denied choices: they are given treatment they do not understand and prescribed drugs without being made fully aware of their effects. Even when under a great deal of stress, they are not informed about the existence of paramedical or support services. It is assumed that Asian women would automatically be supported by their family, and advice is given in ignorance of the fact that at times the families itself may be a source of difficulty.

In the rare cases where Asian women are sufficiently employed in influential positions, services to the Asian community are dramatically improved. An Asian community worker in a women's centre near London, through imaginatively targeting Asian girls and young women on health issues, dramatically increased the number of women demanding breast screening and smear tests. She was so successful that she heard complaints from the local Well Women's Centre all the following week because the women had gone along to demand these checks. She asked if the women had gone back to the clinic; apparently one who was followed up did have a lump in her breast.

> If she hadn't known that she could demand a mammography she would have accepted the doctor's examination and left it at that. But because she knew that there is something called a mammography available for women if they're worried she demanded it. The clinic in fact should have taken it more seriously. They should have seen that there was this large group of women who they hadn't been reaching. (Community Health Care Action, 1989)

In the Subcontinent, in addition to the formal systems of medicine, there exists a wealth of information and cultural practice, generally handed by the older women to the younger, of folk medicine and general health care. Women who came to Britain as part of the first waves of immigration were largely cut off from this valuable resource, although as the Asian communities in this country have added generations, part of the network of information and advice has survived. An example is the practice of body massage of mothers and babies, an everyday therapy on the Subcontinent for relieving both bodily and mental aches and pains, and still practised in varying degrees in the Asian community in Britain. Babies are calmed and soothed by massage, which serves to reinforce the bond between mother and child. Women after childbirth are also massaged, to help them to regain their muscle tone.

There are several community self-help organisations working to improve health care, such as the Leicester Black Mental Health Group. McNaught (1987) describes these groups as 'voicing their dissatisfaction with the health service, responding to gaps in services, trying to meet the need for mutual support, and exploring alternative models and approaches for health care provision'. Such groups, however, are often beset with insecure temporary funding and are not always in a position to employ community health professionals to do all that needs to be done.

As the pressures of living in Britain build up they are beginning to take their toll on the health of Asian women who, more than ever before, are turning to traditional uses of therapy from *hakims*, homeopaths and *pirs*, or priests. This they find preferable to being sectioned at a local psychiatric hospital or being prescribed drugs whose effects they do not fully understand.

The tradition of self-help and self-reliance of these communities in the face of practices which range from general indifference and neglect to outright hostility, preserves, as far as possible, windows of opportunity. Significant numbers of women in Leicester, Leeds and Bradford run their own businesses against all odds. In some cases their client group is exclusively other Asian women as they specialise in Asian clothing, for instance in parts of London, Leicester and Bradford, or more mixed, for example Leeds market where they sell Western-style dress. Asian women medical doctors, lawyers, teachers and other professionals all look to their own community for support in the face of continued discrimination, so competition is ever keener for the same markets. In the Subcontinent where they only have the one barrier, sexism, women are able to achieve in a variety of areas supported and encouraged by the history of women in particular fields of employment. With constant undermining and devaluing of their skills and expertise, and in the absence of positive role models and sustained support, progress in Britain is difficult.

Many women interpret their experiences and situations as the West's attack on Asian families and communities and particularly on Muslims. These ideas began to take hold in the period after the Rushdie affair when the Muslim community internationally felt affronted, and have become still more deeply embedded since the Gulf War and the genocide of Muslims in the former Yugoslavia. In the aftermath of these international events British Asian Muslims have begun to claim their Muslim identity over and above being Asian. This manifests itself in dress and other social behaviour. Men and women have begun to mix less easily in social situations and some women are adopting the *hejjab*, full *burqua* and long skirt rather than *shalwar qumeez*. This new wave seems to cut across class divisions. In some instances, the families who make the biggest compromises in the effort to integrate are the strictest within the family. This is reminiscent of the situation in Saudi Arabia in the 1990s that we saw in Chapter 3: when its contact with the West became strongest and Saudi society felt threatened, it tried to control the most central of its institutions, the mosque, where gender segregation became evident for the first time.

## The Goddess Kali's island

'On Kali's island' – in an ideal world – the role of education is to create chances and widen horizons. Here the education system draws from international sources of learning from past and present. Knowledge is regarded as a common human heritage belonging to all people, so carrying no national or cultural superiority. On Kali's island, the Asian woman can be religious or a non-believer or have a belief system which amalgamates different religious traditions and Eastern and Western philosophies. She can choose to pursue any course of study at any institution, depending only on her ability and aptitude. She can live wherever she likes according to her financial means without giving rise to 'white flight'. She can follow whatever form of medical treatment is most suited to her condition or personal preferences. She can marry whoever she likes and her husband can join her at once. A woman can choose to be married, have children and live in an extended family system, be the head of household, wear dungarees and be a commercial airline pilot, wear *shalwar qumeez* or a sari and *hejjab* and be a television newsreader, be unmarried and practice as a medical consultant, be divorced, live with her children and practise as a lawyer in matrimonial law or as a high court judge, be a Member of Parliament or lead the country irrespective of whether or not she is single, married or divorced. She may be self-employed or be a housewife. She can be an artist or a scientist or indeed choose any career or life-style without being pigeon-holed. In all situations on Kali's island her decisions are well informed.

Chapter 7

# East and West

Mugrib, mushriq, shumal, junoob,
our story's told bohat khoob,
Rich, poor, large and small
None gives us share in all.
Exploitation is the lot of 'wife'
Struggle for freedom is my life.

This book has tried to show, through the lives and aspirations of individuals in the Subcontinent and in a Western town, how Asian women's lives are dominated by patriarchy – and, in many cases, their own efforts to resist oppression – wherever they live.

## The power of patriarchy

Whether women are in seclusion/purdah, whether they have their feet bound or restrict their freedom of movement with stiletto heels, whether their genitals are mutilated or corsets maim their internal organs, or whether they hit a 'glass ceiling' in their promotion ladder, they are subject to societal constraints. Their bodies have become part of the political battleground, and undue attention is focused on the acceptability of their mode of dress, which varies according to cultural norms. In order to justify constraints on women's behaviour, men lean on scriptures or common-sense morality. Notions of family honour are invoked to gain psychological control over women until ultimately they internalise 'respectable' modes of behaviour. Even their family lives are not free from society's moralising and preaching. The seeming failure of men to resolve their relationship with their mothers generates a conflict of love and loathing for the female figure that may remain with them for the rest of their lives. To convince themselves of the inferior nature of women, men have sought the support of science, pseudo-sciences and the supernatural. In extreme circumstances such as war, famine or emigration, when the usual social mores are inapplicable, women are allowed to extend beyond their prescribed roles in defeating the common enemy, but as soon as the society returns to normality, the ground they have gained is reclaimed, and they are restricted as before.

When lineage is passed through the male, great emphasis is placed on the chastity of women. But child-rearing primarily remains the responsibility of women and, like other female roles, it is undervalued and under-supported. Because of their socio-economic or political circumstances, the women who achieve in 'non-female' arenas, are held to be exceptional, thus separating them from women in the mainstream and denying women's achievements generally.

Women's second-class status in most societies across the world is institutionalised. Watching any United Nations conference shown on television confirms the paucity of female heads of state. The democracies in the First World fare little better than the previously colonised 'Third World'. The US, self-professed liberator of peoples from totalitarian regimes, has not yet managed to produce a single white woman president, let alone a black or Asian one.

## Asian women in England

This book has shown how the socio-economic system in Britain, which has largely perpetuated the class position of Asians, has profound effects on the Asian community, which in turn affect gender relations within that community. A statistically insignificant amount of political space is accorded to Asian men in local and national politics. The main political parties may feel justified in criticising the limited involvement of Asian women in the political machinery, without recognising that politics itself still largely excludes women. Further, by not creating opportunities for Asian women and by liaising predominantly with Asian men, especially the so-called community leaders who wield the power to deliver the votes, British politicians give tacit acceptance to the *status quo*.

Political parties should consider positive action to elect Asian women as local and national politicians, just as the Labour Party brought more – white – women into Parliament in 1997. All public policy should be flexible to cater for the needs of its clientele. Services should be adaptable to the cultural and religious requirements of all individuals. To offer the same provision in the face of differing needs is not equitable.

The improvement of the community or its gender relations cannot be left to chance. Leisure for Asian women, which gives them respite from domestic duties, needs to be considered along with educational and career opportunities, social services and health care and adequate housing. Women need to have space in which they can decide their own agenda and express themselves in their own way, whether through their art, for instance, embroidery, singing, dancing, painting their hands with henna or simply relaxing away from the interference of men. They should be encouraged to partake in the mainstream life of the country, including local and national politics. Otherwise the retreat into purdah, in various ways, will continue in Britain to be the only option, rather as it is in Iraq, where a strict Islamic code has been adopted after the 'Allies' destroyed the economic base of the country in the Gulf War.

Despite the rhetoric, most women carry the emotional burden of human societies. World-wide, women spend but a fraction of the wealth they create. In the rare instances where a woman does become head of state, this does not automatically improve the situation for the majority of women in the country. It may be that she succeeded on the terms of male institutions whose continued support she requires to remain in power, so denies her own experience and tacitly accepts women's generally inferior position – as did Margaret Thatcher and Benazir Bhutto.

In Britain, despite the Sex Discrimination Act, the position of women in most professional hierarchies remains low. For Black and Asian women the situation is even bleaker. The position of Asian women everywhere has to be seen not only in the general context of prejudice against women, but also against the background of colonialism and neo-colonialism. Asian women, it is felt, are fundamentally different from the white administrators, teachers and social workers: a group somehow less than fully civilised and who deserve pity and kindly help. During the British Empire the colonial authorities portrayed Asians in general, and Asian women in particular, as powerless and abject victims. This mind-set persists today: any example of extreme behaviour in the Asian community, such as a case of sati, is sensationalised in the media, reinforcing the classic 'otherness' and with it the notion of the inferiority of the Asian woman. Research is needed to determine whether similar attitudes prevail in Canada and the US.

The ultimate legacy of colonialism was the partition of India and the hundreds of thousands of deaths on both sides of the borders. In Britain these divisions are perpetuated through community centre politics. In the meantime Asians in general and Asian women in particular are excluded from their rightful share in the field of employment and service provision. This marginalisation has created a poor, angry and disaffected underclass.

Asian women are subjected to a barrage of cultural constructs which aim to predetermine their roles; these are more difficult to cope with in the West because they are more frequently unfounded. Every girl has to come to terms in womanhood with her own identity, the perception of this identity by others, and the roles which these others seek to define for her. Depending on her politicisation she may, consciously or unconsciously, accept, reject or redefine these externally defined roles. This difficult task is compounded for Asian women in the West, and certainly in Britain, by the societal forces of racism and colonial thinking which constrain her in a way which her own culture may not. The women workers I studied in Pakistan and India were able to carve out careers for themselves even though operating within a patriarchy. They were not burdened with the extra dimension of racist notions of their cultural 'otherness' as 'ethnic minorities', which denies British Asians equal access to services and career opportunities.

Asian women are a part of Western societies, yet they continue to be perceived as 'problems' and not as what they are: a vital new element of a society which has itself been changed by their presence, like adding milk to tea. We all take from and contribute to the new and different society which has evolved in ways which are pertinent and relevant to us as individuals or groups. An exciting range of foods can be bought on any English high street and a chain-store or couture suit may well be influenced by the styles of the Subcontinent. It is possible to costume a television adaptation of a Jane Austen novel from the silks and muslins of the Asian fabric shops, all of them made in the Subcontinent, just as in Jane Austen's life-time.

The one characteristic common to almost all immigrants is a drive to adapt to and succeed in their new circumstances. America, the most powerful nation in the world, is a land of immigrants. So is Singapore, now one of the world's most prosperous economies, which a couple of hundred years ago was a forested island. Without new blood and new ideas, any society will stagnate. There is every advantage to gain from ceasing to waste the talents and energies of a large section of British society. The healthy development of any civilisation depends on its ability to adopt and adapt 'new' ideas; Renaissance Europe flourished by mining Greek and Roman knowledge which had been preserved and developed by the Muslim world.

Asians in the West have, despite the barrage of criticism and racism, managed to create a measure of self-sufficiency; East African Asians, in particular, have prospered in England. Living in run-down inner-city areas, unemployed and in poor housing, many of the Asian parents I interviewed in west Yorkshire have managed to find the money to have private tuition for their children to supplement their state education. Asian parents will pay for alternative health care when the National Health Service fails them; they will buy their own homes when local authority housing is not available.

This energy needs to be usefully channelled and skilfully exploited if we are to avoid producing a generation of Asian women who feel compelled to define their identity in religio-cultural terms epitomised by their mode of dress. The role of education is to create chances and open up opportunities. The experience of many, if not most, Asian women going through the educational system in Britain and pursuing a career in that and other fields is one of frustration, isolation, racial discrimination and alienation.

Professionals, especially in the world of education, should not stereotype or make generalisations. The constraints on successive generations of British Asians are largely being created by the very people whose function it is to serve them. The individual's needs and the circumstances in which she finds herself should be explored before jumping to easy or clichéd solutions about Asian women and their religio-cultural or family traditions. As this book has shown, all are subject to change. None is immutable.

Women in the Subcontinent, who according to the received wisdom about them should be less free and less able to pursue careers, education and independent life-styles, reveal themselves in the interviews reported here as tough, clear-thinking and effective. Women-only professional hierarchies in medicine, banking, and retailing have certainly proved to be an asset to some in the Subcontinent; for others, having a secluded workplace is not an issue and they are able to compete more freely with men. But as this book goes to press, the Prime Minister of Pakistan is seeking to replace the country's legal code with the *Sharia* and already Pakistani liberals and human rights activists are fearful of the impact on women (*Guardian*, 1 August 1998). And in certain regions of India, brides are burned to death in their thousands each year in dowry disputes (Menski, 1998).

For centuries the subordinate status assigned to women has been part of their collective consciousness. But Asian women have a particular story to tell. Colonialism, by looting treasure and cultural artefacts, undermining agrarian and industrial economies and exploiting raw materials, systematically destroyed social and economic institutions. The large pool of landless labourers thus created were available to be exploited as indentured or migrant workers throughout the Empire. Their families, sometimes abandoned, sometimes transported with them, were as affected as the men; these population movements radically changed the fabric of society not only in the countries to which they were carried but also in the land that they left. Communities have been uprooted in search of political stability and economic security. In the words of a nineteenth-century Urdu poet, Mir Taqi Mir:

> Our existence is like a bubble
> This panorama is like a mirage

All over the world, women struggle to make ends meet, but just as a bubble leaves no trace on the water's surface after it vanishes, so are their efforts erased from the pages of history and their search for happiness, justice and equilibrium sinks without trace. Asian women are told that they are passive victims and that their men, especially Muslims, are oppressive tyrants. In this view, both need distinctive treatment: the men require the firm hand of a teacher, social worker or policeman; the women have to be rescued and liberated.

The truth is that their men, once used as cannon- and factory-fodder, are today emasculated by being thrown onto dole queues and having their right to work and provide for their families usurped. They may, if they get a job, be passed over for promotion in favour of a white woman or man. Asian women, who had lost their inheritance rights during the colonial era, and were often left to head the family when their men were taken away, are constantly short-changed in Britain because of a lack of educational, training and career opportunities, and oppressive and racist immigration laws.

While the Western research has focused in detail on women in an English town of high settlement from the Subcontinent, the broad principles have been shaped by the Western belief system of racio-cultural superiority derived from Europe's colonial past (Said, 1993, 1995). Just as the concept and position of women as second-class citizens is defined and refined in accordance with the socio-economic and political needs of a society at any time, so it is with race. Each Western country finds its own way of subjugating Asian women and their regio-cultural backgrounds. This is exemplified by the reporting, as front page headline news in the *New York Times*, of the sati by the eighteen year old Roop Kanwar in India in 1987, as with the incident a few years earlier of a woman stoned to death for adultery in a Middle Eastern country (see Chapter 3). These isolated events become emblems of 'Third World' barbarity enacted against its women. They simultaneously represent universal patriarchy and what Rajan calls 'specific third world religious fundamentalism' (Rajan, 1993). Professional Asian women in the US, for instance, are not immune from the effect of this mode of thinking (Trinh, 1989).

The Second World War brought to an end the old world order of direct European control over its colonies. Nevertheless, patterns developed and perfected during imperialism persist in more subtle ways. Cultural and economic imperialism finds expression through, for example, the marketing of Western style clothing, foods and cosmetics. Along with consumable commodities are presented the Western racio-cultural archetypes which the indigenous populations are encouraged to emulate. The Subcontinent's economic development thus becomes tied up with buying Western products which are paid for via the growth of cash crops for the West's consumption, at the expense of basic domestic needs such as food and building materials. This neo-colonial relationship is sustained through an elaborate system of bondage called 'aid'. The decimation of Indian industry during the British Raj by levying crippling taxation finds its equivalent in the continuing retardation of the the Subcontinent's economy by the ever-present threat of punitive economic sanctions. This is epitomised by the West's reaction to India and Pakistan's decisions to test their nuclear weapons in May 1998. President Clinton's comment, widely reported in the media, that it would be 'nutty' for India and Pakistan to attempt to become nuclear powers, aptly sums up the unequal relationship which has existed between the Subcontinent and the West for some two hundred years.

This book has described how the lives of Asian women are inextricably intertwined in the intricate web of national and international events. Events which continue to shape their lives, across class divisions, through social institutions such as property inheritance, purdah, sati, marriage and divorce, ever since 3000BC. Their present position in the Subcontinent is the same as that of women globally – as subordinate to men. In the West the weakness of their position is exacerbated by the current economic imbalance between the Subcontinent and the neo-colonial powers, and by notions of white racio-cultural superiority dating from the colonial period. The strategies for coping or resisting oppression may vary in East and West, but the struggle is much the same.

## Oppressed Coverage
*Shamshad Khan*

It's not often you give us prime time slot

but make an exception in time of trouble
when you star us on the news
on ITV **and** BBC

bomb blast it was us who did it
famine the result of Islamic rule
demonstrations only of mindless masses
women covered it's got to be oppressive

and it won't be the last time there's confusion
about Muslims and Islam in this nation
whether on radio or TV
rampaging fundo oppressive repressives
you know
even I'm starting to get
a negative picture of me

bomb blasts it was us who did it
famine the result of Islamic rule
demonstrations only of mindless masses
women covered it's got to be oppressive

and whatever the news
you restate your views with such ease
always finishing with a call to prayer
Allah-U-Akbar

any excuse to show us on our knees.

(Copyright Shamshad Khan)

# Glossary

**Anumarana** – a form of *sati*

**Asian** – Commonly used in the West to describe people originally from the Indian Subcontinent or their descendants

**Ayurvedic** – based on the *Ayurveda*, a collection of ancient Hindu medical treatises on the art of healing and prolonging life

**Bakhti** – religious, pious spiritual

**Beesi** – informal banking system

**Begum** – lady, usually a title for a married woman

**Bhangra** – originally a Panjabi folk dance, this has become the pop dance of young Asians in Britain

**Bharat Natyam** – south Indian classical dancing style, originally developed as temple dancing

**Bollywood** – the Indian film industry based in Bombay

**Brahman** – member of the highest or priestly Hindu caste

**Burqua** – all-enveloping outer garment of different shapes; sometimes in one piece resembling a shuttlecock with lace or crocheted piece inserted across the area covering the eyes; sometimes in two, with the lower part shaped like a degree gown and the upper like a cape coming up to the head and tied under the chin, plus two chiffon veils which can be drawn over the face. They vary in length. The 'shuttlecock' is always floor length, the other can range from floor length to knee length depending on fashion.

**Chunari Mahotsav** – thirteenth day after *sati*, when a red veil is ritually placed on the site of the pyre

**Dharma** – way of righteousness

**Dharmastastra** – the science or study of righteousness

**Dowry** – customary gifts bride brings to her husband and his family

**Dulhan** – newly-wed bride, feted for a short-time before assuming her domestic duties

**Duputta** – long draping scarf, sometimes worn over the head

**Ethnic minority** – a group of people defined by a common religious or cultural heritage and living in a country as a minority

**Fatwa** – condemnation by Muslim religious authority

**Filmi** – anything related to or connected with the vast film industry in the Sub-continent

**Gara** – a sari worn by Parsis. It is hand embroidered with a distinctive design to commemorate their exodus from China

**Gharara** – wide trousers gathered at the knee

**Ghazal** – devotional or love poetry, usually sung, in rhyming couplets

**Ghurdamad** – a son-in-law who comes to live with the bride's natal family

**Granth** – sacred scripture of the Sikhs

**Gurdwara** – Sikh temple

**Hajj** – sometimes spelt Haj – a pilgrimage to Mecca required of all Muslims who are able to afford it

**Hadith** – sayings of the Prophet Mohammed

**Hakim** – a herbalist health practitioner

**Halal** – permitted

**Harajin** – once known s 'Untouchable'; lowest Hindu caste

**Haram** – forbidden

**Harem** – living space reserved for women

**Hejjab** – or **hijab** head covering, often a large head scarf

**Izzat** – family, group or personal honour, respect or standing. It can be specifically applied to women's behaviour. Anything which brings in to dispute the good name of an individual or a group: ' face losing.'

**Janhar** – suicide *en masse* at time of catastrophe or conquest

**Kabaah** – square black structure housing at one of its corners a meteoric stone, round which Muslims making a pilgrimage to Mecca circumambulate. It is believed to have been originally founded by the prophet Abraham.

**Karma** – destiny or fate, dependent on one's previous actions

**Kathak** – north Indian classical dancing, developed at the Moghul court

**Lathi** – a long heavy wooden stick used as a weapon in India, commonly by the police

**Levirate** – the practice of a man marrying the widow of his brother

**Mahir** – that part of the dowry which a husband provides for his wife. The actual term is specifically applied to Muslim practice, although a form of dowry to the bride from her husband goes across religious divisions

**Masjid** – mosque

**Memsahib** – a European woman in the Subcontinent

**Muddrussah** – originally 'school' in Arabic – denotes Quranic or Islamic school

**Murdana** – men's area or living space in a house or elsewhere

**Mushairah** – gathering of poets at which they sing and recite their own and other poets' work

**Nawab** – aristocrat – usually applied to Muslim heads of Principalities who were often descendents of Moghul Emperors

**Niah** – intention or commitment used by Muslims both in the specific religious sense and in general

**Odissi** – classical Indian dancing style, developed in Orissa

**Panchayat** – open court system of village elders, governing daily life

**Pir** – a Muslim religious healer

**Pundit** – a Brahman Hindu learned in religion or law

**Purdah** – female seclusion, privacy or veiling

**Putivrati** – a wife who has vowed her devotion to her husband

**Qumeez** – tunic worn over shalwar, which can either be short or long according to fashion

**Quran** – Islamic holy book of divine revelation. Also spelt Koran.

**Quvi** – strong

**Quwaali** – originally religious poetry, usually sung, now used also for love poems

**Raga** – classical Hindu musical form

**Raj** – rule, government: British administration in India before Independence in 1947

**Raja** – male ruler

**Ram** – female ruler

**Sahamarana** – a form of *sati*

**Sari** – length of cloth up to nine yards long, pleated and draped about the body; usually worn over a blouse and petticoat

**Sari-pallu** – the long free end of a sari, worn draped over the upper body

**Sati** – sometimes spelled suttee – the custom of widow-burning on husband's funeral pyre

**Sativrati** – one who has made a true promise – usually a faithful wife

**Shadi hall** – wedding venue

**Selemlik** – men's quarters, or living space

**Shalwar** – trousers, usually with stiff decorative cuffs, which may be baggy or tight according to fashion

**Shariah** – the body of doctrines regulating the lives of Muslims

**Shariat** – court and legal system based on the Islamic Shariah laws

**Sunnah** – Islamic tradition based on the words and actions of the Prophet Muhammad

**Tawaph** – circumambulation seven times round the *Kabaah*

**Tiffin** – copper or brass food carrier, used by English during British Raj to mean 'lunch'

**Umrah** – an optional pilgrimage to Mecca for Muslims

**Yashmak** – face covering worn by women to conceal identity

**Zaeef** – weak

**Zamidar** – originally a tax-collector, now a landlord

**Zenana** – women's living area

# Bibliography

Ackroyd, R: Special health unit for ethnic groups, *Yorkshire Post* p. 13, 12.8.1993

Ackroyd, S and Hughes, J A (1981) *Data Collection in Context*, Longman, New York

Afshar, H ed. (1985) *Women, Work and Ideology in the Third World*, Tavistock Publications, London

Ahmad, W I U ed. (1992) *The Politics of 'Race' and Health*, Race Relations Research Unit, University of Bradford and Bradford and Ilkley Community College

Ahmad, W I U ed. (1993) *'Race' and Health in Contemporary Britain*, Open University Press, Milton Keynes

Ahmed, A S (1993) *Living Islam: from Samarkand to Stornoway*, BBC, London

Ahmed, L (1992) *Women, Gender and Islam*, Yale University Press

Ali, A ed. (1988) *Third World Impact,* Hansib Publications, London

Allen, S: New Minorities, Old Conflicts: Asian and West Indian Migrants in Britain, in *Race and Class*, Vol 17, 1971

Allen, S (1982) *Ethnic Disadvantage in Britain*, Open University Press, Milton Keynes

Allen, S and Barker, eds. (1976) *Dependence and Exploitation in Work and Marriage*, Longman, London

Allen, S and Wolkowitz, C (1987) *Homeworking: Myths and Realities, Women in Society*, Macmillan, Basingstoke

Altekar, A S (1973) *The Position of Women in Hindu Civilisation*, Indological Publishers and Book-sellers, India

Anwar, M (1979) *The Myth of Return: Pakistanis in Britain*, Heinemann, London

Aqueel, N (1993) *The Transition of Asian Girls at 16+*, Asian Women's Resource Association and Calderdale College, Halifax

Asian Woman Killed For 'Having Affair' *Guardian,* 26 September, 1995

Barthes, R (1972) *Mythologies*, selected and translated by Annette Lavers, Jonathan Cape, London

Beck, L and Keddie, N (1978) *Women in the Muslim World*, Harvard Univesity Press, Cambridge Mass

Beddoe, D (1989) *Back to Home and Duty*, Pandora, London

Bhaktivedanta SP, A C ed. (1988) *Bhagavad-Gita As It Is*, Bhaktivedanta Book Trust, Bombay

Bhatti, S: Language Difficulties and Social Isolation: the case of South Asian women in Britain, in *New Community,* Summer 1976, Vol 5

Bradford Heritage Recording Unit (1994) *A Century of Immigration, Destination Bradford*, BHRU, Bradford

Bradford Metropolitan District Council (1984) *District Trends 1984:the Changing Face of Bradford*, Bradford

*Bradford Telegraph and Argus*, 6.7.95

Brindle, D: Ethnic balance rule for hospitals, *Guardian* p.8, 9th December 1993

Brooks, G (1995) *Nine Parts of Desire*, Hamish Hamilton, London

Brown, C (1984) *Black and White Britain: the Third Policy Social Institute Survey*, Policy Studies Institute, London

Butterworth (1967) *Immigrants in West Yorkshire*, The Institute of Race Relations, London

Calderdale Metropolitan District Council (1991) *Ethnic Minority School Leaver Unemployment – an in depth study*, Halifax

Calderdale Metropolitan District Council (1993) *Language Support Service: Annual Project Report 1992-3*, Halifax

Campbell, M and Jones, D (1982) *Asian Youth in the Labour Market: a study in Bradford*, Bradford College

Carby, H V (1982) 'White Women Listen! Black women and the boundaries of sisterhood' in *The Empire Strikes Back: race and racism in contemporary 70s Britain*, University of Birmingham Centre for Contemporary Cultural Studies and Hutchinson

Care plan for ethnic groups, *Yorkshire Evening Post*, p.7, 29.9.1992

Carr, J (1993) *Alibis for Inaction*, City of Bradford Metropolitan Council, Bradford

Castle and Kosack, G (1973) *Immigrant Workers and the Class Structure in Western Europe*, for the Institute of Race Relations, Oxford University Press

Cavendish, R (1982) *Women on the Line*, Routledge and Kegan Paul, London

Chaudhary, V: Language barrier threatens medical treatment, *Guardian* p.6, 12.8.1993

Cleveland County Research and Intelligence Unit (1992) *The Asian Community Survey*, Cleveland

Collective Perspectives, *Feminist Review*, Autumn 1984

Commission for Racial Equality (1984) *Race and Council Housing in Hackney*, CRE, London

Commission for Racial Equality (1985) *Ethnic Minorities in Britain*, CRE, London

Commission for Racial Equality (1985) *Immigration Control Procedures: Report of a Formal Investigation*, CRE, London

Commission for Racial Equality (1985) *Race and Mortgage Lending in Rochdale*, CRE, London

Commission for Racial Equality (1986) *Teaching English as a Second Language: Report of a Formal Investigation in Calderdale Local Education Authority*, CRE, London

Commission for Racial Equality (1988) *Ethnic Minority School Teachers: a survey in eight local education authorities*, CRE, London

Commission for Racial Equality (1988) *Medical School Admission*, CRE, London

Commission for Racial Equality (1991) *Lessons of the Law: A Casebook of Racial Discrimination in Britain*, CRE, London

Conference of Social Economists (1980) *Capital and Class*, London

Cook, G C: Some Medical Problems Affecting the Ethnic Minorities of the UK, J. *Royal Society of Health*, June 1992

Crishna, S (1975) *Girls of Asian Origin in Britain*, YWCA

Deem, R (1978) *Women and Schooling*, Routledge and Kegan Paul, London

Department of Education and Science (1985) *Education for All: The Report of the Committee of Inquiry into the Education of Children from Ethnic Minority Groups*, (Swann Report) HMSO, London

Department of Employment (1995) Racial minorities in the UK Workforce *in Employment Gazette*, London

Department of Health (1991) *The Health of the Nation: a consultative document for health in England*, HMSO, London, quoted in W.I.U. Ahmad (1992), op. cit.

Donnan, H and Webner, P eds (1991) *Economy and Culture in Pakistan: Migrants in Cities in a Muslim Society*, Macmillan, Basingstoke

Dutt, R P (1949) *India Today*, People's Publishing House, Bombay

Eck, D L (1986) *Speaking of Faith: Cross-cultural perspectives on women, religion and social change*, Women's Press, New Delhi

Edwards, M (1967) *British India 1772-1947: a survey of the nature and effects of alien rule*, Sedgwick and Jackson, London

Eggleston, J, Dunn, D and Anjali, M (1986) *Education For Some*, Trentham Books, Stoke on Trent

Female caught behind commercial veil, *Guardian* 26.10.1995

Flamarion, E (1997) *Cleopatra: From History to Legend*, Harry and Abrams, New York

Forster, E M (1936) *A Passage to India*, Penguin, Harmondworth, Middlesex

Fruzzetti, L (1981) 'Farm and Hearth: Rural Women in a Farming Economy' in: *Women, Work and Ideology in the Third World*, ed. Afshar, Travestock, London

Ginsberg, S (1991) 'Legend of the Jews' in *The Myth of The Goddess: Evolution of an Image* ed. by A. Baring and J. Cash, Penguin, Harmondsworth

Gokalsingh, K and Dessanyake, W (1998) *Indian Popular Cinema*, Stoke on Trent, Trenham Books

Goldberg, D A and Rayner, J D (1995) *The Jewish People, Their History and Religion,* Penguin, Harmondsworth

Government Statistical Service (1995) *Labour Market Trends*, HMSO, London

Greenhalgh, P: Ethnic Groups and a Question of Health, *Times* p.17, 9.2.1991

Hall, C: Health Ministry admits neglect of ethnic minorities, *Independent*, p.4, 29.8.1992

Hastings, D and Webner, P (1991) *Economy and Culture in Pakistan: migrants and cities in a Muslim society,* Macmillan, Basingstoke

Hattersley, Roy: article in *Guardian* 1.5.1994

Hawley, J. S ed. (1994) *Sati, the Blessing and the Curse: the burning of wives in India*, Oxford University Press, New York and Oxford

Health Education Authority (1995) *Black and Minority Ethnic Groups in England,* HEA, London

HEFCE (Higher Education and Funding Council for England) (1995) *Special Initiative to Encourage Widening Participation of Students from Ethnic Minorities in Teacher Training*, HEFCE Publications

Hobsbawm, E (1995) *Age of Extremes; the short twentieth century 1914-1991*, Abacus, London

Holy Bible, The King James version (1611)

Home Office (1981) *Report of Select Committee on Racial Attacks*, HMSO, London

Hopkins, A and Bahl, V (1993) *Access to Health Care for People from Black and Ethnic Minorities*, Royal College of Physicians, London

Ikramullah, S (1963) *From Purdah to Parliament,* Cresset Press, London

The Industrial Society (1986) *Women in Insurance Project,* Industrial Society, London

Jain, D ed (1975) *Indian Women,* Ministry of Information and Broadcasting, Government of India, New Delhi

Jain, D ed (1986) *Religion and Social Change*, The Women's Press, New Delhi

Jeffery, P (1979) *Frogs in a Well: Indian women in purdah*, Zed Press, London

Kabeer, N: Do Women Gain from High Fertility? *Journal of the Institute of Race Relations and the Transcultural Institute*, Summer 1975, Vol I

Kabeer, N (1984) *Reversed Realities: gender hierarchies in development thought,* Verso, London

Kalra, S S (1980) *Daughters of Tradition: adolescent Sikh girls and their accommodation to British Society,* Diana, Balbir Publication, Birmingham

Kelsey, B and Kelsey, M (1991) *Sacrament of Sexuality: the spirituality and psychology of sex*, Element, Dorset

Khan, S: Bilingualism in the curriculum, *Multicultural Teaching*, Vol 13 no 1, Autumn 1994

Khan, S (1995) *Equity for the Black Community*, Calderdale Local Education Authority, Halifax

Khan, S (1997) The Importance of Home Language, unpublished paper presented at the Conference on Equality in Education, Leeds Metropolitan University

Khazi, S: *Daily Gang*, Karachi, 23.12.1987

Kosack, G: Migrant Women: the move to Western Europe – a step towards emancipation? *Journal of the Institute of Race Relations and the Transnational Institute*, Summer 1975, Vol I

Leeds City Council Directorate of Education (1994) *The Secondary Black Pupil Achievement Survey 1994: Summary Report*, Leeds

Leeds City Council Directorate of Education (1995) *The Primary Black Pupil Achievement Survey 1995: Summary Report*, Leeds

Leeds City Council, Leeds Entry Assessment: Autumn Intake, 1997

Leghorn, L and Parker, K (1981) *Women's Worth,* Routledge and Kegan Paul, Boston

Lemu, B A and Heeren, F (1987) *Women in Islam,* The Islamic Foundation, Leicester

Liddle, J and Joshi, R (1986) *Daughters of Independence*, Zed Press, London

Lim, S G, Tsutakawa, M, and Donnelley, M (1989) *The Forbidden Stitch: An Asian American Women's Anthology*, Calyx Books, Corvallis

Lipsedge, M (1993) 'Mental Health: access to care for black and ethnic minority people', in Hopkins, Anthony and Bahl, Veena, *Access to Health Care for People from Black and Ethnic Minorities*, Royal College of Physicians of London

Lister, H, Simpkin, M and Jones, M (1994) *Redressing the Balance: Health and inequality in Leeds*, Leeds Health for All, Leeds

Loomis, L R (1942) Introduction to *Plato: Five Great Dialogues*, Van Nostrand, Princeton

Macdonald, J (1976) Women at Work in Britain and the Third World, in *Women, Work and Ideology in the Third World*, Tavistock, London

MacRobbie, A. and McCabe, T. eds (1981) *Feminism for Girls: An Adventure Story*, Routledge and Kegan Paul, London

McNaught, A (1987) *Health Action and Ethnic Minorities:* written for the National Community Health Resource, Bedford Square Press, London

Mares, P, Henley, A and Baxter, C (1985) *Health Care in Multiracial Britain*, Health Education Council, Cambridge

Mather, J and Ayres, C (1981) *Asian Women and Further Education*, EOC Research Project, Manchester

Melman, B (1995) *Women's Orients: English women and the Middle East, 1718-1918*, Macmillan, London

Menski, W (ed) (1998) *South Asians and the Dowry Problem.* Trentham Books, Stoke on Trent

Mernissi, F (1985) *Beyond the veil: male-female dynamics with modern Muslim society*, Al Saqi, London

Mernissi, F (1986) Femininity as Subversion in Eck, D L and Jain, D *Cross-Cultural Perspectives on Women, Religion and Social Change*, The Women's Press, New Delhi

Mernissi, F (1986) Beyond the Veil: Male-female dynamics in Muslim Society, in Eck, D L and Jain, D *Cross-Cultural Perspectives on Women, Religion and Social Change*, The Women's Press, New Delhi

Mernissi, F (1995) *The Harem Within: Tales of a Moroccan Girlhood*, Bantam Books, Torontou, and London

Mihill, C: Health Unit set up for ethnic illness, *Guardian* p. 6, 12.8.1993

Mihill, C: Special Health Unit for Ethnic Groups, *Yorkshire Post*, p.13, 12.8.1993

Miles, R (1989) *The Women's History of the World*, Paladin Books, London

Minnesota Department of Commerce Study (1984) *Should Gender Be Used as an Insurance Rating Variable?* Minnesota Department of Commerce

Mount, F (1982) *The Subversive Family: An Alternative History of Love and Marriage*, Jonathan Cape, London

National Group on Homeworking (1994) *Home Truths: Report No. 2*, NGH, Leeds

Nehru, J (1989) *An Autobiography:* Centenary Edition, Oxford University Press

O'Day, R (1994) *The Family and Family Relations, 1500-1900 England, France, and USA*, Macmillan, London

Oakley, A (1981) 'Interviewing women: a contradiction in terms' in Roberts, H. *Doing Feminist Research*, Routledge and Kegan Paul, London

Omvedt, G (1980) *We Will Smash This Prison: Indian Women in Struggle*, Zed Press, London

Orwell, G (1958) *Burmese Days,* Popular Library, New York

Ozment, S (1983) *When Fathers Ruled,* Harvard University Press

Pahl, J (1989) *Money and Power in Marriage*, Conference of British Sociological Association, London

Pakistan PM to Impose Sharia, *Guardian* p.13, 29.8.1998

Parmar, P (1982) 'Gender, Race and Class' in *The Empire Strikes Back: race and racism in contemporary 70s Britain*, Centre for Contemporary Cultural Studies, University of Birmingham, Hutchinson University Library

Patterson, S: Two Steps Forward, One Step Back?, *New Community*, Vol V No 1-2, Summer 1976

Pike, A: Study starts of ethnic minority healthcare, *Financial Times,* p.8. 29.8.1992

Pollert, A (1981) *Girls, Wives, Factory Lives*, Macmillan, London

Pomeroy, S.B (1976) *Goddesses, Whores, Wives and Slaves: women in classical antiquity*, Hale, London

Rajagopalachari, C ed. (1976) *Mahabharata*, Bharatiya Vidya Bhavan, Bombay

Rajagopalachari, C ed (1976) *Ramayana,* Bharatiya Vidya Bhavan, Bombay

Rajan, R S (1993) *Real and Imagined Women: Gender, culture and postcolonialism*, Routledge, London

Randa, S N (1975) 'Women construction workers in Delhi' in *Women Construction Workers*, ed. V. Majumdar and R.N. Sachdev, Allied Publishers, New Delhi

Ranger, C (1988) *Ethnic Minority School Teachers: a CRE survey of eight LEAs*, Commission for Racial Equality, London

Richardson, D and Robinson, V eds (1993) *Introducing Women's Studies*, Macmillan, London

Roberts, J and Khan, S (1983) Education in a Multi-Racial Society: a report on a series of five community meetings held in Leeds in February and March 1983, Leeds Community Relations Council, Leeds

Sachdeva, S (1993) *The Primary Purpose Rule in British Immigration Law*, Trentham Books, Stoke on Trent

Said, E (1993) *Culture And Imperialism*, Chatto and Windus, London

Said, E (1995) *Orientalism: Western Conceptions of the Orient*, Penguin, Harmondsworth

Sarup, M (1986) *The politics of multicultural education*, Routledge and Kegan Paul, London

Scarman Report (1981) *The Brixton Disorders 10-12 April 1981*, HMSO, London

Shaarawi, H (1986) *Harem Years: the memoirs of an Egyptian feminist,*1879-1924 translated and introduced by Margot Badran, Virago Press, London

Shaheed, F and Mumtaz, K (1987) *Women of Pakistan: two steps forward, one back*, Vanguard, Lahore

Singh G P A (1993) *Asian Teachers in British Schools: a study of two generations,* Multilingual Matters, Clevedon

Singh, A V S (1993) *Women's Studies in India: Information Resources, Services and Programmes,* Sage Publication, London and Delhi

Sinha, G P (1975) Women construction workers in Bihar in *Women Construction Workers,* ed. V. Majumdar and R.N. Sachdev for Allied Publishers Ltd, New Delhi

Smaje, C (1995) *Health, 'Race' and Ethnicity: making sense of the evidence,* Kings Fund Institute, London

Smithers, R: Labour set to back divorce changes, *Guardian,* 17.6.1996

Spender, D ed (1983) *Feminist Theorists: three centuries of women's intellectual tradition,* The Women's Press, New Delhi

Standing, H: Resources, Wages and Power: the impact of women's employment on the urban Bengali household, *Journal of the Institute of Race Relations,* Vol I 1975

Stevens, M. The Fate of Women's Land Rights, Gender, Matrilinearism and Capitalism in Remban Negeri Sembilan, Malaysia, *Journal of the Institute of Race Relations,* Vol I, Summer 1975

Survey pinpoints deprived ethnic minority, *Yorkshire Post* p.16, 19.10.1992

Tavernier (1925) *Travels in India,* Oxford University Press Vol I

Tellis-Naik, J B (1983) *Indian Womanhood: then and now – situations, efforts, profiles,* Sat Prachar Press, Indore

Tharu, S and Lalita, K eds (1991) *Women Writing in India, 600 BC to the Present: Vol.1, 600BC to the early 20th century,* Pandora, London

Thompson, E.J (1928) *Suttee: a Historical and Philosophical Inquiry into the Hindu Rite of Widow-Burning,* Allen and Unwin, London

Tower Hamlets Borough Council (1995) *Staff Equality Audit,* Tower Hamlets Borough Council, London

Townsend, P, Davidson, N and Whitehead, M (eds) (1992) *Inequalities in Health. The Black Report: the health divide,* Penguin, London and New York

Trinh, T M (1989) *Woman, Native, Other,* Indiana University Press

Tully, M (1995) *The Heart of India,* Penguin, Harmondsworth

UNISON (1997) *Pall Mall: the unacceptable face of contracting,* UNISON, London

Visram, R (1992) *Women in India and Pakistan: the struggle for independence from British rule,* Cambridge University Press

Walker, B (1968) *An Encyclopaedic Survey of Hinduism: Vol II Hindu World,* Unwin, London

Walker, S and Barton, L eds (1983) *Gender, Class and Education,* Falmer, Lewes

Wallman, S (1979) *Ethnicity at Work,* Macmillan, London

Walser, G (1968) *The Persian Empire: studies in geography and ethnography of the Ancient Near East, edited by Ernst Herzfeld from the posthumous papers* by Gerald Walser, F Steiner, Wiesbaden

Ward, L Fair Exchange, *Bradford Telegraph and Argus,* 6.7.1995

Watterson, B (1991) *Women in Ancient Egypt,* Alan Sutton Publishing, Stroud

Weir, A and Mackintosh, M: Towards a Strategy for Women, *Feminist Review,* November 1982

Wiffin A: Ask the family, *Guardian,* 17.4.1996

Williams, L O (1988) *Partial Surrender: Race and Resistance in the Youth Service,* Falmer Press, London

Wolpert, S (1989) *The New History of India,* Oxford University Press

Woolley, L and Moorey, P R S (1992) *Ur of the Chaldees,* Herbert Press, London

Yamani, M (ed) (1996) *Feminism and Islam: Legal and literary perspectives,* Garnet, Reading

Young, K, Wolkowitz, C and McCullagh, R eds (1981) *Of Marriage and the Market: women's subordination in international perspectives,* CSE Books, London

# INDEX